TIMELESS BOOKS OF TRUTH

When you're seeking a book on practical spiritual living, you want to know that it is based on an authentic tradition of timeless teachings and that it resonates with integrity.

This is the goal of Crystal Clarity Publishers: to offer you books of practical wisdom filled with true spiritual principles that have not only been tested through the ages but also through personal experience.

Started in 1968, Crystal Clarity is the publishing house of Ananda, a spiritual community dedicated to meditation and living by true values, as shared by Paramhansa Yogananda and his direct disciple Swami Kriyananda, the founder of Ananda. The members of our staff and each of our authors live by these principles. Our work touches thousands around the world whose lives have been enriched by these universal teachings.

We publish only books that combine creative thinking, universal principles, and a timeless message. Crystal Clarity books will open doors to help you discover more fulfillment and joy by living and acting from the center of peace within you.

How to Be a Success

Paramhansa Yogananda

How to Be a Success

Paramhansa Yogananda

Crystal Clarity Publishers
Nevada City, California

Crystal Clarity Publishers, Nevada City, CA 95959
ISBN: 978-1-56589-231-6

Printed in Canada
1 3 5 7 9 10 8 6 4 2
Designed by Crystal Clarity Publishers

Library of Congress Cataloging-in-Publication Data
Yogananda, Paramhansa, 1893-1952.
  How to Be a Success / by Paramhansa Yogananda.
     p. cm.
  Includes index.
  ISBN 978-1-56589-231-6 (trade paper, indexed, photos of
yogananda)
  1. Success. I. Title.
  BF637.S8Y55 2008
  294.5'44 — dc22

                                        2008010453

www.crystalclarity.com
800.424.1055
clarity@crystalclarity.com

Contents

Publisher's Note 9

1 The Attributes of Success
(early version of *The Law of Success*) 13

2 What Is Your Aim in Life? 33

3 Eliminating Habits of Failure 43

4 Developing Habits of Success 59

5 Tools of Success 71

     • Concentration 73

     • Will Power 75

     • Magnetism 83

6 Success in the Workplace 91

     • Finding Your Vocation 95

     • How to Satisfy Your Employer 100

     • How to Select Your Business Associates 108

7 Stories of Success 113

8 "Seek Ye First the Kingdom of God" 123

Index 135

List of Illustrations 146

About the Author 147

Further Explorations 149

"Your success in life does not depend only upon natural ability; it also depends upon your determination to grasp the opportunity that is presented to you. Opportunities in life come by creation, not by chance."

—Paramhansa Yogananda

Dear Reader,

In this book Yogananda shows you how to develop the unlimited powers that come from innermost forces of your being.

Paramhansa Yogananda came to the United States from India in 1920, bringing to the West the teachings and techniques of yoga, the ancient science of soul awakening. He was the first master of yoga to make his home in the West, and his *Autobiography of a Yogi* has become the bestselling autobiography of all time, awakening fascination in Westerners with the spiritual teachings of the East.

Yoga is the ancient science of redirecting one's energies inward to produce spiritual awakening. In addition to bringing Americans the most practical and effective techniques of meditation, Yogananda showed how these principles can be applied to all areas of life.

The articles included in this book are taken from several sources: the lessons he wrote in the 1920s and 1930s, articles of his that appeared in Inner Culture and East West magazines published before 1943, and the booklet The Attributes of Success published in 1944. Most of what is included here is not available elsewhere.

Our goal in this book is to let the Master's spirit come clearly through, with a minimum of editing. Sometimes sentences, redundant in the present context, have been deleted. Sometimes words or punctuation have been changed to clarify the meaning. Great care was taken not to change any of the original intention.

We hope you will use Yogananda's words as stepping-stones to the success you are seeking.

Crystal Clarity Publishers

How to Be a Success

CHAPTER 1

THE ATTRIBUTES OF SUCCESS

Is there a power that can reveal hidden veins of riches and uncover treasures of which we have never dreamed? Is there a force that we can call upon to give health, happiness, and spiritual enlightenment? The saints and sages of India taught that there is such a power. They uncovered truths that we have overlooked or forgotten, and these truths will work for you, too, if you give them a fair trial.

Your success in life does not depend only upon natural ability; it also depends upon your determination to grasp the opportunity that is presented to you. Opportunities in life come by creation, not by chance. They are created by *you*, either now or at some time in the recent or distant past. Since you have earned them, use them to the best advantage. You can make your life much more worthwhile, now and in the future, if you focus your attention on your immediate needs and use all your abilities and available information to fulfill them. You must develop *all* the powers that God gave you, the unlimited powers that come from the innermost forces of your being.

Your thoughts will inevitably bring you either to failure or to success — *according to which thought is the strongest.* Therefore, you must thoroughly believe in your own plans, use your talents to carry them out, and be receptive so that God can work through you. His laws work at all times, and you are always demonstrating success or failure, according to the kind of thoughts that you *habitually* entertain. If your trend of thought is ordinarily negative, an occasional positive thought is not enough to change the vibration to one of success.

Don't run after your problem constantly. Let it rest at times, and it may work itself out—but see that *you* do not rest so long that the whole proposition eludes you. Rather, use these periods when your mental and physical efforts are in abeyance to go deep into the calm region where your inner Self reigns. When you are attuned with your soul, you will be able to think correctly about everything you do; if your thoughts or actions have gone astray, they can be realigned.

The Dynamic Power of Will

Along with positive thinking, you must use will power and continuous activity in order to be successful. Everything that you see is the result of will, but this power is not always used consciously. There is mechanical will as well as conscious will. The dynamo of all our powers consists in volition, or will power. Without volition, we cannot walk, talk, work, think, or feel. In order *not* to use this energy, you would have to lie down and not move at all.

Even when you move your hand, you are using will power. It is impossible to live without using this force, but it must be wisely directed to achieve success.

To create dynamic will power, determine to do some of the things in life that you thought you could not do. Attempt simple tasks first. Then, as your confidence strengthens and your will becomes more dynamic, you can undertake more difficult accomplishments. Be sure that you have made a good selection, then refuse to submit to failure. Devote your entire will power to accomplishing one thing at a time; do not scatter your energies or leave something half done to begin a new venture.

Use your will power to perfect yourself. You must depend more and more upon the *mind* because it is the creator of your body and your circumstances. Carrying a thought with dynamic will power means entertaining that thought until it assumes an outward form. When your will power develops that way, and when you can control your destiny by your will power, then you can do tremendous things.

I have just given you three important rules for making your will power dynamic:

> 1. Choose a simple task or accomplishment that you have never mastered and determine to succeed in it.

2. Be sure you have chosen something constructive and feasible, then refuse to consider failure.

3. Concentrate on a single purpose, using all abilities and opportunities to forward it.

You must train yourself to use conscious, not mechanical, will, and you must be sure that your will power is used constructively, not for harmful purposes or trifling things. Always be sure that what you want is right for you to have, then use all the force of your will power to accomplish your object, always keeping your mind on God—the Source of all.

Life Energy and Will Power

The human brain is the storehouse of life energy. This energy is constantly being used in muscular movements, the working of the heart, lungs, diaphragm, cellular metabolism, chemicalization of blood, and in carrying on the telephonic sensory motor system of the nerves.

Life energy is used by the mind, the emotions, and the body, for it is involved in all processes of thought, feeling, and physical activity. *The greater the will, the greater the amount of energy in any body part.*

One of the greatest enemies of will power is fear. Avoid it both in thought and in action. The life force that is flowing steadily through your nerves is squeezed out when the nerves become paralyzed by fear, and thus the body's vitality is diminished. Fear paralyzes your will power. When fear comes, the brain discharges the message to all the organs. It paralyzes the heart, disturbs the digestive forces, and causes many other physical disturbances. You must be cautious but never afraid.

Failure as a Stimulant

Even failure should act as a stimulant to your will power, and to your material and spiritual growth. Weed out the causes of failure, and with double vigor launch what you wish to accomplish. *The season of failure is the best time for sowing the seeds of success.*

The bludgeon of circumstances may bruise you, but keep your head erect. Always try *once more*, no matter how many times you have failed. Fight when you think that you can fight no longer, or when you think that you have done your best, until your efforts are crowned with success.

Every new effort after failure must be well planned and charged with increasing intensity of attention and dynamic will power.

A and B were fighting. After a long time, A thought, "I cannot fight any longer." B said to himself, "Just one more punch!" He gave it, and down went A. You must be like that. Give that last punch. Use your will power.

The successful person may have had more difficulties than other people, but he doesn't mention them. He rejects the thought of failure at all times.

Unless you know how to transfer your attention from failure to success, from worry to calmness, from mental wanderings to concentration, from restlessness to peace, from peace to conscious divine bliss within—then all life's labors have been in vain. If you have attained this control, then the purpose of life has been gloriously fulfilled.

Suppose you have failed so far? It would be foolish to give up the struggle, accepting failure as the decree of "fate." It is better to die struggling than to give up the struggle while there is still the possibility of accomplishing something more, for after death your struggles will soon be renewed in another life. Success or failure comes only by acquirement—only as the result of what you have done in the past *plus* what you do now. You must stimulate all the success thoughts of past lives until they are revitalized and overrule the influence of predominant failure tendencies.

Analyze Yourself

Another secret of progress lies in self-analysis. Introspection is a mirror in which to see portions of your mind which otherwise would remain hidden from you. It is never too late to diagnose your failures and to assess your good and bad tendencies. Analyze what you are, what you wish to become, and what tendencies or shortcomings are impeding you. Decide what your deep and secret task is—your mission in life—so that you can make yourself what you should be and what you want to be. In working toward that end, use initiative as well as will power.

What is initiative? It is the creative faculty within you, a spark of the Infinite Creator. It may give you the power to create something no one else has ever created. It urges you to do things in new ways. The accomplishments of a person of initiative are as spectacular as a shooting star. He makes what has appeared impossible become possible, by utilizing the great inventive power of Spirit.

You alone are responsible for yourself. Your friends and the world of activity will not answer for your deeds when the final reckoning comes. No one has the power to detract from your happiness unless you allow the adverse thoughts and actions of others to affect you. You have duties in the world, in the sphere where your karma (action) has placed you. Help to work out your salvation by serving your fellow man. Like the impartial rays of the sun, you must spread rays of hope in the hearts of the poor and the forsaken, kindle courage in the hearts of the despondent, and light new strength in the hearts of those who think they are failures.

Learn to see God in all people. When you begin to feel your oneness with every human being, you will know what divine love is. When in service we forget the little self, then will we see the one measureless Self of God flowing through us.

Most of us are inclined to assist ourselves, and to analyze others coldly, guided by our prejudices. We should reverse this by assisting others and coldly analyzing *ourselves.* When you do analyze someone else, the most important thing is to keep your mind unbiased. Your unbiased mind must act like a clear mirror, held steady, and not oscillating with hasty judgment. Then, you will see an undistorted image of any person reflected within you.

Control Your Habits

Until you are master of yourself, able to command yourself to do the things that you should do but may not want to do, you are not a free soul. This freedom is not a small thing to acquire—*in that freedom lies the germ of eternal freedom.*

It is not your passing thoughts or brilliant ideas but your everyday habits that control your life. Habits of thought are mental magnets; they draw to themselves specific objects relative to the quality of their magnetism. Material habits attract material things.

Bad habits are temporary, misery-making grafts upon the soul. The law of nature is that if you are a little less evil than good, your evil will be taken away by the greater power of good; and if you have a little less good than evil, your goodness will gradually be absorbed by the greater number of evil tendencies.

If a bad habit bothers you, weaken it by avoiding everything that occasioned or stimulated it, *without concentrating upon it in your zeal to avoid it.* Then, divert your mind to some good habit, and keep it energetically engaged in cultivating that habit until it becomes a part of yourself.

There are always two forces warring against each other within us. One tells us to do things we should not do, and the other urges us to do things we *should* do and to do things which seem difficult. One is the voice of evil, and the other is the voice of God.

If you are able to free yourself from bad habits, and if you are able to do good because you *want* to do good and not because doing evil will bring you sorrow, then you are truly progressing. It is only when you discard your bad habits that you are a free individual.

Reaching the Source of Will

I have mentioned some of the attributes you must cultivate in order to achieve success—positive thoughts, dynamic will, self-analysis, initiative, and self-control—but these are only the first steps. Many popular books stress one or more of these, but do not give credit to the Power which is behind them. Self-analysis should lead to a better understanding of the inner Self. The cultivation of dynamic will should flower in attunement with the divine will.

Will is the power that moves the cosmos and everything living in it. It was God's will that shot the stars into
space. It is His will that holds the planets in their orbits
and directs the cycles of birth, growth, and decay.

When Jesus said, "Let Thy will be done," what did
He mean? He meant that when man attunes his will with
God's will, which is guided by wisdom, then he is using
Divine Will. You will not know what Divine Will is until
you have developed your own will and learned to harmonize it with the Supreme Will. This divine contact is gained
through meditation.

Divine Will has no boundaries; it works in all bodies,
in all things. It can change the course of destiny, wake the
dead, and change the orbits of the planets. You must exercise
your will in every undertaking, until it drops its delusion
of being human will and becomes one with all-powerful
Divine Will. You only need to *know* that you already possess it, and that the image of God is within you.

When guided by error, your human will can mislead
you, but when guided by wisdom, it is attuned to the Divine
Will. Unfortunately, God's plan for you often becomes
buried beneath the conflicts of human life, and you lose the
guidance which could save you from the chasm of error.

Only by using your will power rightly can you contact God's will.

The Ocean of Abundance

Just as all power lies in His will, so all spiritual and material gifts flow from His boundless abundance. In order to align yourself with it, you must eradicate from your mind all thought of lack or poverty. The Universal Mind is perfect, it knows no lack. To reach that never-failing supply, you must create a consciousness of abundance—even if you do not know where your next dollar will come from. When you refuse to be apprehensive, and do your part and rely on God to do His, you will find that mysterious forces will come to your aid, and your constructive wishes will materialize.

Since God is the source of all mental power and prosperity, do not will and act first, but contact God first and thus harness your will and activity to the right goal. As you cannot broadcast through a broken microphone, so you cannot broadcast your prayer through a mental microphone that is disordered by restlessness. By deep calmness you must repair your mental microphone and increase the receptivity of your intuition, so that you can broadcast to Him and receive His answers.

The Value of Meditation

When you are calm and attuned to constructive vibrations, how can you use your mental microphone to reach Him? The right method of meditation is the only satisfactory way.

By the power of concentration and meditation, you can direct the untold power of your mind to accomplish what you desire, and you can guard all doors through which failure may enter. All men and women of success have devoted much time to deep concentration and meditation—though some of them may never have used the word "meditation" to describe their mental processes. They were people who could dive deeply into their problems and come out with the pearls of right solutions. If you learn how to withdraw your attention from all objects of distraction and place it upon one object of concentration, then you will know how to attract at will what you need.

When you want to create something important, sit quietly, calm your senses and your thoughts, and meditate deeply upon what you want to do or acquire. You will then be guided by the great creative power of Spirit. After that you must use all material resources to bring about whatever you wish to accomplish.

What Constitutes Success?

I have discussed some of the attributes of success and have told you how to use them. But do you know what constitutes *success*? What does the word mean to you? Real success comes by so increasing your mental efficiency that you can supply the things you need in life — but remember, there is a great difference between things that you *need* and things that you *want*.

To lead a successful life you must first have a dominant purpose. That purpose must be the right one for *you*, then all the powers of God will guide you in your plans and activities. When you have resolved definitely upon a purpose in life, you must then make everything serve that purpose. Extraordinary talent is not as necessary as an unswerving determination and unfailing application of effort.

Does fulfillment of the purpose you have chosen constitute success? What *is* success, anyway? If you have lots of health and lots of wealth, but lots of trouble with everybody, including yourself, you have very little. The entire purpose of life becomes futile if you cannot find happiness. Therefore, success must be measured by happiness — by your ability to remain in harmony with cosmic laws — rather than by health, prestige, or wealth.

Determine to Be Happy

God neither punishes nor rewards you, for He has given you the power to punish or reward yourself by the use or misuse of your own reason and will power. It is *you* who have transgressed the laws of health, prosperity, and wisdom and punished yourself with sickness, poverty, and ignorance. Do not continue to carry your burden of old mental and moral weaknesses acquired in the past, but burn them in the fires of resolution, and become free.

Happiness depends to some extent upon external conditions, but chiefly upon conditions of the inner mind. In order to be happy, one must have good health, an efficient mind, a prosperous life, the right work, a thankful heart, and above all, an all-rounded, all-accomplishing wisdom.

A strong determination to be happy will help you. Do not wait for your circumstances to change, thinking that in them lies the trouble. Do not make unhappiness a chronic habit, for it is anything but pleasant to be unhappy, and it is blessedness for yourself and others if you are happy. When you are unhappy, you forget the days when you were happy, and when happiness comes, the days of unhappiness seem to leave forever. Sunny days would not be appreciated if there were no cloudy days, so happiness cannot be appreciated without having experienced unhappiness.

Find His Power Within

Use constructively the power which you already have, and more will come. Move forward with unflinching determination, using all the attributes of success. Tune yourself with Cosmic Power. Then you will possess the creative power of Spirit. You will be in contact with Infinite Intelligence, which can guide you and solve all problems. Power from the dynamic Source of your being will flow through you so that you will be creative in the world of business, the world of thought, or the world of wisdom.

When you absolutely convince God that you want Him above all else, then you will attune with His will. When your will continues to want Him no matter what comes to take you away from Him, then you are acting according to God's will.

The power of truth is yours. If you make a determined effort, you will no longer walk in fear and uncertainty on the path of life. There is a Power which will light your way, which will bring you health, happiness, peace, and success, if you will but turn toward that Light. Swim in the ocean of vastness, peace, and limitless happiness beyond dreams — *within yourself!*

My Divine Birthright

I will seek God first, and make sure of my actual contact with Him; then, if it is His will, all things — wisdom, abundance, and health — will be given as part of my divine birthright, since He made me in His image. I want prosperity, health, and wisdom without measure, not from earthly sources, but from God's abundant, all-possessing, all-powerful, all-bountiful hands.

Chapter 2

What Is Your Aim in Life?

Most people live almost mechanically, unconscious of any ideal or plan of life. They come on earth, struggle for a living, and leave the shores of mortality without knowing why they came here, and what their duties were.

No matter what the goal of life is, it is obvious that man is undermined by needs that he struggles to satisfy. It is very important to concentrate on one's true needs and not to create lots of useless extra desires. Man must differentiate between real needs and unnecessary "necessities."

The person who is wrapped up with his unnecessary necessities and physical luxuries forgets to concentrate on the little needs of his body and on his great need of developing mental efficiency and divine contentment.

He buys new automobiles and new clothes on the installment plan, so that he is always in debt and forced to spend all his time in unsuccessful attempts at making money. He has no time to develop his mental efficiency or to cultivate inner peace because he is enslaved to the demands of Tyrant Physical Luxury habits.

Prosperity does not consist just in the making of money; it also requires developing the mental efficiency by which man can consistently acquire health, wealth, wisdom, and peace.

In the search for success one must concentrate on *needs* and not on *wants*. It is well that man does not get everything he wants, and that the Cosmic Law does not grant wishes that would result in harm. A child may ask his father to catch him a beautiful poisonous snake, but the father does not fulfill such a dangerous wish. The Divine Law also denies the gratification of harmful, though momentarily pleasurable, desires. Of course, as God's child, man, with the gift of free will, can, and often does, persist in his longing for things which seem delightful in the beginning but are harmful in the end.

The greater the need, the greater the likelihood that it will be filled. Before you can get what you *want*, you must develop the power to get at will that which you need.

What are your real needs? —Food for body, mind, and soul, shelter, prosperity, health, the power of concentration, a good memory, an understanding heart, friends, wisdom, and bliss are some human needs. Plain living, high thinking, and cultivating real happiness within oneself in order to make others spiritually happy are also real needs.

True happiness is lasting because it is spiritual in nature, whereas the "happiness" based on sense pleasure soon turns to sorrow. Making the senses serve the needs of body and mind leads to true happiness; indulging the senses brings nothing but misery. A desire for a pleasurable sense object is often mistaken for a natural *need* instead of an artificially created *want*. *Wants* must not be multiplied; instead, concentration must be directed toward filling real *needs*, or securing actual necessities.

As a rule, the attention is absorbed by unnecessary *wants* and constantly increasing desires. All desires for the gratification of needless *wants* must be stamped out.

Focusing the attention on one *need* at a time is the first step in the right direction. Determine your greatest *need*, including all the factors of life and true happiness; then devote all your attention and energy to attaining your objective by the quickest method.

Do not wander aimlessly, lost in the jungle of life, with your happiness constantly bleeding away from the thorn-pricks of new desires. You must find the goal of life, and the shortest road to lead you there. Do not travel unknown roads, picking up new troubles. Too much wrong ambition is just as bad as too much passive contentment.

As human beings, we have been endowed with needs, and we must meet their demands. As man is a physical, mental, and spiritual being, he must look after his all-round welfare, avoiding one-sided over-development. To possess wonderful health and good appetite, with no money to maintain that health or to satisfy that hunger, is agonizing. To have lots of health, lots of wealth, and lots of trouble with yourself and others, is pitiable. To have lots of health, wealth, and mental efficiency, but lack of peace and no knowledge of the ultimate truth, is useless and dissatisfying.

Most people think that they are prosperous only when they have plenty of money, but real success means to have all things at your command—the things that are necessary for your entire existence. Very few people know the real meaning of "needs." If the need is boiled down to certain definite things, then the need can be easily satisfied.

Money is not a curse. It is the manner in which you use money that is important. You ask a dollar bill, "Shall I buy poison with you?" It doesn't answer, but if you misuse this brainless dollar, it will punish you. When you use it rightly, it gives you happiness. There is no saint who does not use money in his work. Whoever eats has to pay for the food, and it is better to be able to buy your food than to live on charity.

Most people spend all their mental energy trying to make money, and some who are successful die of heart failure before they are able to secure happiness. The entire purpose of life becomes futile when you cannot find true happiness. When wealth is lost, you have lost a little; when your health is lost, you have lost something; but when your peace is lost, all is lost.

You must increase the strength of your body and then increase the strength of your mind. The best way to increase mental power is to try to accomplish something worthy every day. Try to do the things you have been told you could not do. The more you improve yourself, the more you can be a friend to all.

When you make up your mind to do something, let the earth and sun fly away from you, but do not give up. You are the child of God—you are just as good as the greatest man on earth. You must have your will power so balanced that you can stick to a thing until you succeed.

First, carefully choose your work. Take your time in deciding what vocation to follow. You must like your vocation if you expect to succeed. If you have not found something that you like, you must search for it. When you make up your mind, stick to your resolution.

When we think that we have to do too much at one time, we become very discouraged. As the clock cannot tick 24 hours away in one minute, so you cannot do in one hour what takes 24 hours to accomplish. Live each present moment completely, and the future will take care of itself. Fully enjoy the wonder and beauty of each instant. Practice the presence of peace. The more you do that, the more you will feel the presence of that power in your life.

Millions of children are started on the path of life without a destination. They act like little wind-up toy engines, running without a track, only to smash up against anything that comes across their path. Such aimless journeys in life are the lot of most people because in early life they were not started toward the right goal, nor were they properly equipped with systematic powers to help them keep moving on their definite paths. On this stage of life most people act like puppets, played on by environment, prenatal instincts, and destiny. They do their duties in life as if in a somnambulistic state.

You should determine your life's path by analyzing your inclinations in early childhood to discover your inborn interests. Once you find your path, try to use all the creative moneymaking methods at your command. Your methods, however, must be in alignment with your idealism, or you may gain money but not happiness.

Wake up! It is never too late to analyze what you are and what your deep-secret tasks are, so that you can make yourself what you should be. You have talents and power that you have not used. You have all the power you need. There is nothing greater than the power of mind. Resurrect your mind from the little habits that keep you worldly. Smile that perpetual smile—the Smile of God. Smile that strong smile of balanced recklessness, that billion-dollar smile that no one can take from you.

CHAPTER 3

ELIMINATING HABITS OF FAILURE

OBLITERATING MALIGNANT SEEDS OF FAILURE AND ILL HEALTH

It is man's reaction to his various experiences—how he faces his tests in the school of life—which indicates how far he has advanced toward perfection. His reactions to everyday experiences not only affect his progress toward ultimate freedom, but also determine his success or failure and his health or sickness for many incarnations.

Like some physical diseases which send their roots deep into his body, the evil effects of man's wrong actions, unless destroyed, become a part of his conscious, subconscious, and superconscious minds and are felt not alone in one lifetime, but in many lives.

What Causes Good or Ill Fortune?

The failures and successes of everyday life become rooted in the mind. Unless they come to fruition or are worked out by wisdom, they bear seeds that the soul must carry into another incarnation as tendencies and traits. These stubborn ghosts of the past hide in the recesses of your mind, and emerge suddenly to help or hinder, according to the circumstances confronting you. These hidden seed tendencies can cause people to fail in their undertakings, in spite of their conscious efforts.

During the war, Henry Ford nearly lost his whole fortune. He had acquired great wealth because he had been prosperous in former lives, but his mind held seed thoughts of fear of failure because of failures in past lives. When conditions during wartime were unfavorable to his line of business, his failure seeds sprouted and almost caused his financial ruin. If he had allowed himself to become truly discouraged, he would have lost everything. By a superhuman effort of will, he fought off the brutal business competitors who were bent on destroying his company. His success consciousness of the past was reinforced by his initiative in this life, his trained business judgment, his knack for choosing the right co-workers, his perseverance, and his daring.

To summarize: financial success depends upon one's earning ability in past lives, and one's initiative and persevering quality of will in this life.

Actions of the Past and Present Affect Our Lives

If the success tendency from past lives and the efforts to succeed in this life are weak, then the chances of financial success in this incarnation are almost negligible. If a person's success tendency from the past is strong, and his present life is marked by inactivity and inertia, then he will either be born into a wealthy family or suddenly inherit a fortune.

The individual who has a strong prosperity consciousness from a past life and makes a strenuous effort to earn money in this life succeeds in all his ventures; such a person seldom loses an investment and has unfailing business judgment. If one begins with a poverty tendency from previous lives but wants to overcome it in this life, he has to struggle uphill in order to succeed. He may either become prosperous late in life or die struggling. But his efforts will not have been in vain, for his next incarnation will be dominated by the success karma resulting from those struggles.

Those who accept failure as the decree of fate are foolish, for success or failure is the result of acquirement either in the present or in the past. If you did not acquire wealth in the past, or if you did acquire it and lost it, dying with the consciousness of your loss, you will be reborn in poverty. By trying hard to overcome your handicap, you stimulate the dormant success consciousness of past lives, until it overshadows the influence of the failure tendencies.

The Will Is Man's Most Effective Weapon

A man cannot be an absolute failure unless he permits fear of failure to exert a paralyzing influence over him.

Friendly success tendencies are ready to help the individual who puts out unflinching efforts; inimical failure tendencies can crush the one who is resigned to "his fate." These are his invisible friends and his unseen enemies. If he rouses his will by repeated judicious efforts, he will awaken the success tendencies sleeping in the chamber of subconsciousness. The will is the weapon for vanquishing failure. Constant use of the will keeps it keen-edged and ready to serve one faithfully. The power of a strong will guided by divine wisdom is unlimited. To its possessor nothing is impossible.

Man carries within himself the seeds of past errors, but he also carries within the seeds of all fulfillment. Under favorable conditions these germinate, and their growth helps to choke the weeds of failure. Financial success in all lives is not impossible to one who knows how to destroy the tendencies of failure by the power of super-concentration.

How to Abolish Want

The only possibility of abolishing want in the world lies in the willingness of successful people to aid failures by helping them overcome their past karma and stimulating their initiative. Some people satisfy their craving for wealth by impoverishing their fellow men; others fail to share their prosperity. Their selfishness is responsible for much suffering in the world. It is deplorable that people who ride in Rolls Royces often ignore the needs of mental and physical cripples who have never received the help that would enable them to help themselves.

If a wealthy man who has acquired success by overcoming his failure tendencies becomes lazy or ignores the needs of others, he may lose his wealth through poor investments or attract poverty to himself in the next life. Rich people who disregard the sufferings of others are reborn with a craving for luxuries but no means to satisfy that craving.

The Importance of Meditation

A man striving for permanent success must meditate every morning and night. When the peace rays of superconsciousness pierce his restlessness, he must concentrate these rays in the brain and mind, scorch the lurking seeds of past failures, and stimulate the seeds of success.

In other words, during meditation the yogi feels the power of concentration in the will center at the point between the eyebrows, and also experiences a feeling of complete peace throughout his body. When he wants to scour from the brain cells the seeds of past failure or sickness, he must direct that peace-and-concentration power to be felt in the entire brain. In this way the brain cells become impregnated with peace and power, and their hereditary chemical and psychological composition is altered.

If failures invade you repeatedly, don't get discouraged. They should act as stimulants to your material or spiritual growth. The period of failure is the best season for sowing the seeds of success. Weed out the causes of failure, and launch with double vigor what you want to accomplish. The bludgeon of circumstances may beat you, but keep your head unbowed. Death in the attempt to succeed *is* success; refuse to harbor the consciousness of defeat. Try always once more, no matter how many times you have failed. When you have done your best and think you can do no more, persevere one minute more in the race for success.

Every new effort after a failure must be well planned and charged with increasing intensity of attention.

Malignant seeds of past karma (action) can be roasted and destroyed only by the fire of persistent effort. Most people give up hope just when the balance of good karma is slowly stooping toward them to give its fruit, and thus they miss their reward.

For the purpose of burning seeds of lurking and chronic diseases, the body-battery charging Energization Exercises* must be practiced with deep concentration, and followed by the Hong Sau technique* of concentration and the AUM technique* of meditation. In practicing these techniques, the consciousness of health, energy, and power must be kept predominant. When this power is felt throughout the

---

* For more information on these techniques, contact Crystal Clarity Publishers.

body as an unquenchable flow of vitality, it must be concentrated in the brain and mind uninterruptedly for a long time. In this way the vital power will destroy all lurking disease tendencies from the past.

If you have an inferiority complex, remember that success, health, and wisdom are your rightful heritage. Your sense of weakness may have had its inception in one or more factors. It can be overcome by determination, courage, common sense, and faith in God and in yourself.

If you are firmly convinced you are a failure, change your mental attitude at once! Be unshakable in your conviction that you have all the potentiality of great success. At times you may find it helpful to recall your mental reactions on occasions when you were unsuccessful in some undertaking.

Practice the Hong Sau technique of concentration faithfully and regularly, and consult your spiritual teacher.

You may find it necessary also to change your mental and physical environment in order to install the proper habits of thought.

After you begin to experience success, act with wisdom and perseverance, no matter what happens, until you demonstrate that you've succeeded as you believed you would.

OVERCOMING FEAR AND FAILURE

The phenomenon of fear is a mental poison, unless it is used as an antidote, a stimulus to spur an individual to calm caution. Fear produces a malignant magnetism which draws to itself the objects of fear, as a magnet draws pieces of iron. Fear increases all our miseries. It intensifies and magnifies our physical pain and mental agonies a hundredfold. Fear is destructive to the heart, nervous system, and brain. It is destructive to the initiative, courage, judgment, common sense, and will power.

Fear contaminates the subconscious mind, and the subconscious mind in turn can completely destroy the willing efforts of the conscious mind. Fear throws a veil over intuition, and shrouds the almighty power of your confidence and the soul's all-conquering power.

Uproot Fear and Thoughts of Failure

Failures and successes remain deeply rooted in the conscious, subconscious, and superconscious minds of one life. Unless released by fruition or wisdom, they accumulate, and at death, travel beyond the grave. Successes and failures are carried to another life as seed tendencies. These past seed tendencies, though generally hidden in one life, begin to manifest themselves when favorable germinating elements arrive.

When something is threatening to hurt you, do not sit idle—do something calmly, do something quickly, do *something*, mustering all the power of your will and judgment. Will is the motive power which works the machine of activity.

Fears of failure or sickness are cultivated by constantly revolving them in the mind until they become rooted in the subconsciousness, and finally in the superconsciousness. From there, fear begins to germinate and fill the conscious mind with fear plants, which bear fruits with poisonous consequences.

If you are unable to dislodge the haunting fear of ill health or of failure, divert your attention by reading interesting books which absorb your attention, or even indulge in harmless amusements. The mind will forget to haunt itself with fear; with new energy, then, you can take up the shovels of various mental strategies and dig out the roots of failure and ill health from the soil of your life.

Uproot fear by forceful concentration upon courage, and by shifting your consciousness to the absolute peace within. Once you have uprooted fear, get busy with methods to acquire prosperity and health.

Fearlessness Is a Cardinal Virtue

Associate with healthy and prosperous people who do not fear sickness or failure. There is a deep-seated reason for chronic ill health and repeated failures. Idlers do not succeed. The self-indulgent suffer, or gradually turn their bodies into hibernating pits of concealed disease germs.

To an unseeing materialist, a disease might appear to be inherited, or the result of a physical law. The doctor says that the father or grandfather had tuberculosis, and that is the reason the son has it. But the spiritual doctor, who traces the deeper causes of chronic diseases and unjust suffering, finds that certain so-called hereditary diseases are not transmitted from one soul to another due to physical reasons. He says that the unborn soul carrying a tubercular tendency from a previous life is drawn to a family where there is tubercular infection.

Of course, tuberculosis can be produced in a healthy body by disregarding physical and hygienic laws. No person, however healthy, good, or prosperous, can be sure of his future unless he has destroyed all seeds of past lives.

Do not fear accidents or disease if you have had them once; rather, be afraid of fear, for fear may bring repeated accidents or disease, and fearlessness will avert them in all probability, or at least neutralize their power.

Death Is a Deliverer

Do not be afraid to die, for death is a deliverer, and you will not die twice. When death comes, then the cause of fear is removed. When suffering is intense, death delivers us from all pain and mental suffering.

Kill fear by knowing that you are protected behind the battlements of God's Eternal Safety—that you are safe even when death dances at your door. God's protecting rays can burn the menacing clouds of doomsday, calm the waves of trials, and keep you safe even if you are on the battlefield of life with bullets of trials relentlessly flying. Without God, your life, health, and prosperity are not protected, even if you hide in a hygienic castle of opulence, surrounded by impregnable trenches.

When fear comes, tense and relax, exhale several times. Switch on the electricity of calmness and nonchalance. Let your whole mental machinery awaken and actively hum with the vibration of will. Then harness the power of will to the cogwheels of fearless caution and continuous good judgment, which must continuously revolve and produce mental solutions for escaping your specific, impending calamity.

Chapter *4*

DEVELOPING HABITS OF SUCCESS

Father Divine, this is my prayer: I care not what I may permanently possess, but give me the power to acquire at will whatever I may daily need. O Father, Mother, Friend, Beloved God, I will reason, I will will, I will act; but guide Thou my reason, will, and activity to the right thing that I should do.

Habits are mental mechanisms which enable us to act automatically, leaving our consciousness free for other duties. A habit is formed by several attentive repetitions of an action.

Some people require much time to form mental habits of health, prosperity, and the acquirement of wisdom. Actually, the time needed for this purpose can be shortened. Slow or rapid habit formation depends on the general state of health, on the condition of the nervous system including the brain cells, and on the type of habit-forming methods used. Most people are halfhearted in their thoughts and actions; hence they do not succeed. A mental habit, in order to materialize, must be strong and persistent.

For instance, the prosperity or health habit must be cultivated by prosperity or health thoughts until results are apparent. An unfailingly wholesome, courageous mental attitude is absolutely necessary to the attainment of one's needs and wants. Failure to prosper and be healthy is due unquestionably to weak mental habits of prosperity and health.

While an inattentive, scatterbrained idiot requires a long time for the formation of even a simple habit, an intelligent, purposeful individual can easily form a good mental habit in a trice, by the mere wish. Therefore, if you have a mental, physical, or spiritual habit that impedes your progress, rid yourself of it now—do not put it off.

Affirm: "I am healthy," or "I am wise." The positive affirmation must be so strong that it completely crowds out any subconscious, discouraging, negative enemy-thoughts that may be whispering to you, "You fool, you will never succeed. You are a failure; wisdom is impossible for you." You must *know* that whatever you wish strongly, you can materialize in short order.

In practicing affirmations, the spiritual aspirant must be unfailingly patient. Believe you are inherently healthy when you want good health; believe you are inherently prosperous when you want prosperity; believe you are inherently wise when you want wisdom—then health, prosperity, and wisdom will manifest themselves in you.

Change the trend of your thoughts—cast out all negative mental habits. Replace them with wholesome, courageous thought habits, and apply them in daily life with unshakable confidence.

Human lives are governed not by weak resolutions, but by habits. When people are used to good health, prosperity, and a high standard of living, all these seem to come easily. Similarly, poverty and failure come to those who are used to them.

Good or bad habits are performed easily and naturally, bringing about good or bad results. Success and failure are habits. Therefore, if you are used to poverty or sickness, you must learn to get used to prosperity and health instead. If failure, sickness, and ignorance are your constant companions, nothing but lack of will prevents you from enlisting the aid of success, health, and wisdom to drive them away definitely and permanently.

Success, health, and wisdom are the natural attributes and habits of the soul. Identification with weak habits and thoughts, and lack of concentration, perseverance, and courage are responsible for the misery people suffer.

Perform little duties very well. Do you know that you have been using only five or six per cent of your attention in your vocation? You ought to use one hundred per cent concentration in doing your work henceforth. All good work is God's work, if you perform it with the divine consciousness. Only work done with a purely selfish motive is material. In earning money, always think that you are doing so for your fellow beings, even if you have no family. Destroy the false division between material and spiritual work.

Be in love with your present work, but don't remain contented forever with what you are doing. You must progress and try to be the very best in your profession. You must express the limitless power of the soul in anything you take up. Every position you hold will be the stepping-stone to a higher one if you strive to climb upward. You must constantly create and produce new success, and not become a business automaton.

The stages of success consist of the following:

1. The choice of a good material or spiritual vocation that suits you.

2. The performance of that work with attention, love, and interest.

3. Continued interest and superhuman patience in your work.

4. The thought of constant progress to neutralize the tendency toward mechanical habit.

5. Finding the Kingdom of Success.

All unsuccessful people are either ignorant of this law or consciously violate it.

Remember that opportunity in life comes by creation and not by chance. It is created by you, either now or in the near or distant past. If you haven't opportunity now, create it by your will, which is divine will, and it shall come to you. It never comes of itself or through good luck.

Success is for the hardworking man, the man of creative ability, the one who knows how to economize. Success is for the man who asks opinions of financial experts before he invests his money. Success is for the man who tries harder to make money after each failure. Success is for the man of incessant working ability.

Success comes to the man of character and regularity. Success comes to the man who does not rest on his laurels. Success comes to the man who performs little tasks well. Success comes to the man who advertises his business rightly and sells the best articles. Success comes to the clear-thinking man, who throws himself earnestly into his work, unafraid of failure.

Success comes to those who make money by making others more prosperous. Success comes to those who spend for God's work with as much spontaneity and pleasure as they do for themselves.

Learn to spiritualize service and to do work that gives the best service to mankind. Make service rather than money your goal, and you will see the entire plan of your life change. You will never be left out.

Most people cannot balance the material and the spiritual life. You must remember that the spiritual man needs money, and the material man cannot be happy without God. Work with God-consciousness. The material man works, but he works and acts with the consciousness that he is the doer, and makes himself miserable with his likes and dislikes.

When business principles are not based upon truth, they are bound to bring misery and suffering.

Purge your consciousness of the selfishness of luxury. Enjoy more luxury in your soul, and decorate yourself with the knowledge and wisdom and love of God. Learn to live simply, and live by a common principle, looking out for the good of others, serving others. Unity can never come if there is selfishness in the heart.

The one-sided businessman, forgetful of his other duties in life, is not the truly successful man. It requires great skill to live life rightly and successfully. He who keeps his engagement only with money is left behind by God.

Destroy the desire for luxury. Learn to use less expensive things in an artistic way, while believing that you are a child of God and that you have all the prosperity of God and the earth behind you. As a child of God—and especially when, by meditation, you change from a prodigal son to a true son of God—you will know that whatever God has, you also have.

1. Reduce luxuries.

2. Think of yourself as a child of God.

3. Think of all nationalities as your brothers.

4. Seek prosperity for yourself and for others.

5. Develop the creative thought of success every day after deep meditation.

Those who seek prosperity for themselves only are bound to be poor for some time, or to suffer from mental inharmony. Those who see the world as their home and who work for group or world prosperity, start the subtle forces working to lead them to their legitimate prosperity. This is the surest secret law of success.

Prosperity does not depend only upon creative ability, but upon your past actions, and also upon the subtle law of cause and effect, which has the power to distribute prosperity equally to all without exception. Those who rouse this astral power of positive prosperity succeed wherever they go. Therefore, seek prosperity, not only for yourself and your family, but for a wider group of friends, for your country, and for the whole world.

CHAPTER 5

TOOLS OF SUCCESS

CONCENTRATION

It does not take long to develop good mental habits. In fact, by exercising strong will, mental habits of health, success, or wisdom may be formed at once. By concentrating on legitimate necessities with perseverance, courage, and faith in God and oneself, one can materialize them at will.

Mental efficiency depends upon the art of concentration. Man must know the scientific method of concentration by which he can disengage his attention from objects of distraction and focus it on one thing at a time. By the power of concentration, man can use the untold power of mind to accomplish that which he desires, and he can guard all doors through which failure may enter. All men of success have been men of great concentration, men who would dive deeply into their problems and discover the pearls of right solutions. Most people are suffocated by distractions and are unable to find the pearls of success.

However, one may be a man of concentration and power and may dive deep into the sea of problems, but still may not find the pearl of success. There are many men who have powerful concentration, but they do not know where to find success. This is where another factor in acquiring prosperity comes into consideration.

Most people live almost mechanically, unconscious of any ideal or plan of life, and without any apparent knowledge of spiritual truth. You must never forget that an important part of your equipment is your purpose in life. The whole world stands aside for the person who knows where he is going and is determined to get there. When you have resolved definitely upon a purpose in life, you must make everything serve that purpose.

The goal of your material life should be maximum business efficiency, peace, health, and general success. Material prosperity consists in acquiring the mental efficiency by which you can gain all these things at will. Great wealth does not necessarily bring health, peace, or efficiency, but acquirements of efficiency and peace are sure to bring balanced material success.

Do not expect to be successful in all your attempts the first time. Some ventures may fail, but others will succeed. Success and failure are interrelated. One cannot exist without the other. With concentrated energy you must approach your nearest problem or duty, and do your utmost to accomplish whatever is needed. This must be your philosophy of life.

WILL POWER

A strong will, by its dynamic force, creates a way for its fulfillment. By its very strength, the will sets into motion certain vibrations in the atmosphere. Nature, with its laws of order, system, and efficiency, then creates circumstances favorable to the individual who exercises will power. Will derives its strength from an honest purpose, lofty motives, and the noble concern to do good for the world at large. A strong will is never stifled—it always finds a way.

Know that anything others do, you can do also. Once I was having dinner with friends. Everything went well until the Roquefort cheese was served. In India we eat only freshly made cheese, so I viewed the little green specks of mold in the cheese with great suspicion. My soul rebelled against it, and my brain cells warned me to have nothing to do with it. But as I looked at my American friends eating the cheese, I mustered courage and took a lump of it into my mouth.

No sooner had it landed there than all the aristocratic delicacies that had preceded it rebelled. There was great clamor and commotion within me, and they let me know that if "Mr. Roquefort" joined them in the stomach, they would all leave the body. I dared not open my mouth, but just nodded in answer to my host's question of whether I liked the cheese! Then, as I looked intently at the faces of my friends eating Roquefort cheese pleasantly, I suddenly made up my mind. Concentrating deeply, I told my brain cells, "I am your boss; you are my servants. You shall obey me—this foolishness must stop." The next minute I was enjoying "Mr. Roquefort's" company pleasantly, and now he always receives a warm welcome when he enters my "hall of digestion."

A *wish* is a desire that you think cannot be fulfilled. *Will* means desire plus energy, or "I act until that desire is fulfilled." How few people actually *will*! You must not use your will power wrongly; your will must be guided by wisdom.

In this life people are following many pathways to one common goal. Some want money, some want health, and others want fame. Various are the desires, but few have the power to accomplish what they wish. How desires come and go in your brain! Do you realize that? When desires corrode your heart, and when you feel it is impossible for you to fulfill them, they are called *wishes*. Sometimes you hear someone say, "I wish I were the King of Egypt," or something else just as impossible. Those are wishes that you know cannot be fulfilled.

Many people think that they shouldn't use their own will power, but it is not possible to avoid using the will. In order to eat, you use your will power; in order to move, you use your will power. When the power to will leaves the body, one dies. The only time you cannot use your will power is when you are under the influence of chloroform.

If you are afflicted with a chronic case of indifference, make up your mind at once to "snap out of it." Be merry—think of something amusing until you find yourself bubbling over with laughter. Exercise self-control: learn to substitute, at will, joy for sorrow, love for hate, courage for fear, openmindedness for prejudice.

Do you know why people fail? It is because they give up. I often say that if I had no job, I would shake the whole world so that it would be glad to give me a job just to keep me quiet. You must *exercise* your will power. If you make up your mind and go like a flame, everything will be burned up in your path. The man of realization walks where bullets fly, with the Divine Will behind him.

Rouse this will power from the vale of ignorance. How can you develop it? Take up one little thing that you think you cannot do. Try with all your might to accomplish that one thing. Then, when you have accomplished that, go on to something bigger and keep on exercising your will power. If your difficulty is great, say: "Lord, give me the power to conquer all my difficulties." You must *use* your will power, no matter what you are, or who you are.

You must *make up your mind.* Use this will power both in business and in meditation.

This will power lies buried within you, and if you use it, there is nothing that you cannot accomplish. It is will power that has created everything—even your body. It is the will that leads you from one desire to another until with all your might you try to succeed. How few people develop that will power!

Carrying a thought with dynamic will power means thinking that thought until it emerges from the brain and takes shape. When your will power continuously develops that way, when you can heal others by your will power, and when you can control your destiny by your will power, you can say to a mountain, "Go into the depths of the sea," and it will be so. Tremendous things you can do!

It isn't what you own, but what you can acquire at will, that is real prosperity. A yogi may not have many material possessions, but by his ability to focus his mind, he can create at will the financial success he needs. (Of course, the yogi does not entertain selfish desires; his only wish is that God's love reign in his soul forever.)

When your will is attuned to wisdom, it is guided by Divine Will. That is what Jesus meant when he said, "Let Thy will be done."

Lazy people think that prayer alone can solve all their difficulties, but you must exercise your will power—strive to attune it to the Divine Will. When your will revolves continuously around a certain thing, it becomes DYNAMIC will. This is the will that Jesus and all great saints have had.

Behind your will is the will of God. Before you will to do a thing, reason as to what you should do. Make sure that you are directing your will toward accomplishing something good and helpful to you. Don't be passive. Those who are passive have converted themselves into stones. Your will was given to you so that you might use it and become a conqueror. Remember, in your will is the will of God.

Say to yourself: I will do everything with my own will, which is a reflection of divine will within me.

In your heart you must love nothing more than God. If you want God, you must use your will to cast away from your heart everything but God. If you want God, nothing wrong can touch you. Remember, you only want one thing: "May Thy love shine forever on the sanctuary of my devotion, and may I be able to awaken Thy love in all hearts." That is my only prayer. I don't even pray for my body. I don't want to enjoy God by myself, but I want to establish the consciousness of God in the hearts of men.

So remember, dear friend, that the greatest will is to will for God alone. God is imperishable and with God every good will come. Develop your will power. Turn your will power away from desires, and know this life is but a dream. Make up your mind to will for God.

Again and again you must send the shells of your prayer and will power to break the ramparts of God's silence. He is castled behind silence, but if you send shell after shell of meditation and concentration, that wall will break and God's glory will burst forth.

Man's will can work within the boundaries of his own little circle of family, environment, world conditions, and destiny, but Divine Will can change the course of destiny, wake the dead, and change the course of the solar or stellar systems. By deep meditation and by wisdom-guided, unflinching, never-discouraged determination, when we can revolve our will around all our noble desires with success, then our will becomes Divine Will.

Therefore, for absolute control of your life and for destroying the roots of failure due to prenatal and postnatal causes, you must exercise your will in every undertaking, until it leaves its mortal delusion of being human will and becomes all-powerful, Divine Will. You do not have to *acquire* this Divine Will—you need only to know that it is yours already.

Pray: "Thou art our Father. We are made in Thine own image. We are sons of God. We neither ask nor pray like beggars, but *deman*d as Thy children, wisdom, salvation, health, happiness, and eternal joy. Naughty or good, we are Thy children. Help us to find Thy will in us. Teach us to use Thy gift of human will in attunement with Thy wisdom-guided will. Teach us to use our will guided by wisdom."

MAGNETISM

You should learn to be magnetic. Everybody possesses the power of magnetism, which is the power by which you draw things to you—the right husband, the right wife, the right business, and so on. If your magnetism is not right, you will draw the wrong people or things. You must learn to develop that fine quality of magnetism by which you can draw to yourself the things that you desire and that are good for you.

Each human being is a medium through which God's magnetism flows, but material desire, revenge, hatred, and an inferiority complex tamper with that magnetism. Do not obstruct that power.

Meditation is the laboratory in which you know that God and His magnetism are with you. Wherever you go, scatter kindness. Let your heart be charged with God, your feet charged with God, your eyes charged with God.

There is within us a magnetic force by which we attract those who have a living relationship to our magnetic power. A human being cannot attract a stone because a stone has no relation to a human being. We know that an ordinary magnet has a certain range and power. Small magnets draw small things. Larger magnets draw larger objects. The human magnet draws according to its power of attraction. Some people attract physical things, some attract mental things, and some attract spiritual things. It depends on what kind of a magnet one wishes to be.

We must develop two kinds of magnetism—one to attract God, and another to attract our material necessities. If we use all of our magnetism to gain material things, sooner or later we shall become disillusioned. It is true that God gave us bodies and we must look after them, but if we first develop spiritual magnetism, it will guide us in the proper ways to supply all our material needs.

Keep your body free from poisons in order to have magnetism. If your body is filled with poisons, you will find that your energy is more or less bound within you. Try to clean out those poisons. If you are clean within, then all your energy can be displayed through your eyes, your face, and your body.

You must pay attention to your diet. Raw food produces magnetism. Coconut produces lots of magnetism. Beets, spinach, and lettuce are full of vitality and give you magnetism.

Too much meat causes you to lose your magnetism because animal magnetism tampers with your spiritual magnetism. Meat causes you to concentrate upon the physical plane too much, and you tend to attract physical companions instead of spiritual ones. Meat also produces abnormal sex life. If you eat a little bit of meat, it won't hurt you, but if you make a habit of eating it daily, it will destroy your magnetic qualities. Eat good meat substitutes, more nuts and nutmeat combinations.

Too much protein and starchy foods retain the poisons in the body. Eating freely of fruits and vegetables can help you to develop magnetism. Fruits are even more magnetized than vegetables. They are filled with sunshine and vital energy. Overeating is bad. Fasting is very good, as it gives the stomach a rest.

Your eyes and your whole body will be magnetized by the kind of food you eat.

We must develop physical magnetism in order to have a body that is strong and can obey our commands. Recharging the body with energy develops great magnetism.[*]

To acquire mental magnetism, we must do everything with deep concentration. People who have reached the top of any profession or business have great magnetic power. If one is a slave to any of the senses, he loses magnetism. If he has control over the senses, he develops magnetism. To develop and maintain an even mind without getting emotional is the way to magnetic living. Emotionalism must be converted into power and be governed by wisdom; then one has great magnetism.

---

[*] Yogananda developed a series of exercises, called the Energization Exercises, for consciously recharging the body with energy. Contact Crystal Clarity Publishers for more information on these exercises.

Every time you are looking, or listening, or lifting your hands, you are throwing out magnetic current. If you are absent-minded, you have no magnetism. When you send a thought, you are sending energy with it. If you are thinking one thing while doing something else, then your energy is divided. When you are fully attentive to what you are doing, then you are developing magnetism.

To be firm is magnetic; to be just is magnetic; to be kind is magnetic.

We must be careful with whom we associate because we are continually exchanging magnetism with other people through our thoughts, through shaking hands, and through looking into the eyes of another person. As soon as we shake hands with someone, a magnet is formed. The person who is the stronger gives his vibration to the other person. We become like the people we mingle with, not through their conversation, but through the silent magnetic vibration that goes out from their bodies. When we come within the range of their magnetism, we become like them.

If a man wants to become an artist, he must associate with artists. If he wants to become a good businessman, he must associate with successful businessmen. If he wants to become a spiritual giant, he must associate with devotees of God.

One can develop cosmic magnetism by thinking of God and saintly people. By concentrating deeply on a certain personality, one can attract that personality. That is why one should think only of great individuals. If we concentrate our thoughts on wicked people, we will attract their qualities unless we are stronger than they are. If our whole heart is with someone, we draw all the defects and all the good qualities of that person.

A magnet has a positive and a negative pole through which it draws to itself pieces of iron or steel within a certain range. When a magnet is rubbed against a piece of non-magnetic iron or steel, the latter also becomes magnetic. People, too, can become magnetized through close association with magnetic personalities to whom they give their deep, loving, and respectful attention. They should first decide what kind of magnetism they want and then choose the particular people who possess it.

For instance, if you are a failure and you want success, associate and shake hands as much as possible with those who have attained success in their business, art, or profession.

In shaking hands, two magnets are formed: the upper, spiritual magnet with the two heads, and the lower, physical magnet with the two pairs of feet as poles. The junction of the hands in the handshake forms the common neutral point as well as the curve for the upper and lower magnets.

What happens when a spiritual man who is a failure, and a prosperous businessman who is spiritually weak, attentively shake hands? Through the two pairs of feet, forming the two poles of one magnet, they exchange physical qualities; through the two heads, forming the two poles of another magnet, they exchange mental qualities. If such men come in close mental contact, besides shaking hands frequently and attentively, the businessman will become more spiritual and the spiritual man will become more prosperous, by virtue of the upper magnet. They exchange their bad qualities also, through the power of the lower magnet formed by the feet. Both the spiritual man and the businessman may be affected in their vocational qualities.

Divine magnetism is the power of all powers. When our prayer bursts from our heart and God relinquishes His vow of silence to speak to us, then we have gained divine magnetism. We must use our time to develop spiritual magnetism in order to attract the Imperishable. Develop the power to attract the highest, and then we can easily attract all lesser things.

We must detach ourselves from this physical residence, the body. Each of us is a spark of the Infinite. We must differentiate between the perishable and the imperishable. Anything that belongs to the body is perishable; anything that belongs to the mind is semi-perishable; anything that belongs to the soul is imperishable.

Stay in tune with the Divine Magnetic Power. Think of God so constantly that He will be with you wherever you go. Then all your good desires, even those formed in the distant past, will materialize.

CHAPTER 6

SUCCESS IN THE WORKPLACE

The main purpose of business should be service, not only money making. The store that gives the best service and the best products is the one people like. Remember that you must serve in order to make others happy.

The law of prosperity is not governed by the law of selfishness, but by the law of unselfishness. Each one of us must live for others. In supporting yourself, you must also support others.

Enter heart and soul into whatever you do, and never become stagnant in your environment. There are two kinds of environment you must watch carefully—your outer environment and your inner environment. By changing your outer environment you may find better success in your work, but don't change unless you are certain that the new situation will be better for you than the place you already work.

Select your vocation in accordance with your inner interest, instinctive inclination, and intuitive meditative guidance. Do not try to seek success in a business that you hate.

It is all right to hold small jobs temporarily, but to die in such positions is a sin against your creative ability. You must let inexperienced newcomers hold small, insignificant jobs, while you, after gathering experience in such jobs, must attain superior positions.

Most people spend their lives desiring to do something perfectly, such as playing the piano or painting, but are too lazy and careless to put forth the effort required to reach perfection in the given activity. They excuse themselves by saying, "I had no time to practice or to find a good teacher, and anyway, I am not a genius." Extraordinary talent is not as necessary as unswerving purpose and unfailing effort. Most people fail to attain their material, mental, and spiritual desires because of lack of definite purpose and sustained effort.

If you want to be an artist or a businessman, you must associate with the best artists and businessmen you can find. By association, I mean intelligent attention, and loving and interested communion. If you are interested in great people in order to learn their ways, they will be interested in you. If you cannot meet great people, you can at least read their books and learn from their successful business experiences.

In order to be a spiritual man, you must associate with a person of the highest spiritual realization, and you must meditate more and more deeply.

Remember that the greatest responsibility in business lies with you, and your awakened creative ability. All difficulties can be overcome only by your continued planning and persistence. Refuse to acknowledge defeat, and you will win. If you don't succeed in the business you are in after trying for some time, then try something else, and keep on trying until you succeed in something. Try to do well in the line of business with which you have experience.

FINDING YOUR VOCATION

You cannot remain stationary—you will either go forward or backward. The way best suited for your life combines your idealism and your practicality.

Suppose you have started on the path of a traveling salesman. You try your utmost, work hard, think and plan, but you do not succeed. Analyze yourself, and you may find that since childhood you have wanted a little vegetable garden and a quiet home where you could reflect, drink peace, and occasionally paint a picture of the landscape. Perhaps this childhood desire to be a farmer and an artist came percolating up from a prenatal existence, or was strongly suggested to you by someone. Your enthusiasm and ambition may have been prejudiced by the impulse of being a farmer. Then why should you try to go against your already formed tendencies?

Most people form their innate heart's desire from the age of three to twelve, but they aren't aware of it. Watch yourself carefully and discover an undercurrent of some definite desire running under the current of your many desires. That underlying desire which has been with you always, coaxing you to listen to it, is the real archangel of success that you should follow.

If your vocation does not satisfy your heart, it is not the right path for you. If you want to reach the abode of lasting peace and happiness, you should pursue whatever path your heart's desire tells you to follow. People are never happy traveling in the wrong direction.

You must also be practical and use your common sense in everything. The person who follows an artistic path, paved after his heart's desire, may satisfy his aesthetic hunger, but may not be productive enough to meet his family's physical hunger!

Remember that where there is a will there is a way. The way best suited for your life may be a compromise between your idealism and practical life. For example, do not give up your desire for gardening, even if you can only have a garden in your backyard and have to go to a city to make money. Have your home in the country, if possible, and spend your weekends finding peace in your garden work.

Play Your Part Well

Besides discovering your innate ambition and learning how to build your moneymaking methods around it, you must do something every day that will satisfy the Cosmic Plan for which you were sent here. Most people are unhappy because they forget to harmonize their earthly, learned duties with the duties demanded by the Cosmic Plan. The Cosmic Plan demands that you satisfy your soul by including in your own happiness the happiness of the most needy ones.

Every day try to help uplift physically, mentally, or spiritually suffering people, as you would help yourself or your family. If, instead of living in the misery-making selfish way, you live according to the laws of God, then, no matter what small part you may be playing on the stage of life, you will know that you have been playing your part correctly, as directed by the Stage Manager of all our destinies. Your part, however small, is just as important as the biggest parts in contributing to the success of the Drama of Souls on the Stage of Life. Make a little money and be satisfied with it by living a simple life and expressing your ideals, rather than make lots of money and have worries without end.

How to Overcome Trials

Trials do not come to you to destroy you, but to help you better appreciate God. God does not send those trials. They are born of your own making. All you have to do is to resurrect your consciousness from the environment of ignorance. Environmental troubles are born because of your conscious or unconscious actions in the past, somewhere, sometime. You must accept the blame for them, without developing an inferiority complex.

You must say: "I know that Thou art coming! I shall see Thy silver lining. In this tumultuous sea of trials, Thou art the Polestar of my shipwrecked thoughts." Why are you afraid? Remember, you are not a man or a woman. You are an Immortal Being.

Even as Jesus could manifest his love and when sorely tested, say, "Father, forgive them, for they know not what they do," so must you forgive your exacting trials and say, "My soul is resurrected. My power is greater than all my trials because I am the child of God." Thus, your mental powers will expand, and your cup of realization will be big enough to hold the Ocean of Knowledge. Then you will be happy and prosperous.

My Own Experience

I loved philosophy and religion from my boyhood, and I made up my mind to establish my own schools and institutions and never hold a job under anybody. It would have been folly on my part to become a railroad man, as was planned for me. I started on my path with infinite confidence that I would succeed, and I did succeed. My success was due to strong determination, and confidence in the guidance of the Heavenly Father in everything I undertook. My effectiveness came through God and creative thinking principally, and very little through human training.

As I headed toward my goal, I tried to succeed in different lines of endeavor. When I saw that I succeeded in all the things I undertook, then I fully launched myself into the greatest undertaking of my life—the founding of spiritual organizations. I started my first work in a little mud hut with three or four others in Calcutta, and finally established a palatial school in India, and a heavenly home in America, with thousands of followers.

I share these things, not to indulge in self-praise, but in order to demonstrate that the above suggestions came from the heart of my own successful experience, and not from theories about success. I hope that if a weak and humble person like myself can accomplish something with which to serve his brethren, you, who are perhaps stronger than I was in the beginning, can surely do something for your success that will also include the success of others.

How to Satisfy Your Employer

Every employer is looking for trustworthy, wholehearted employees who will work not only for a salary but who will take as much intelligent, creative, and industrious interest in the development of the business as the founder of the business himself. The employer and the employee both have a common goal—the real success of the business they have undertaken together. Both of them are servants working for one cause.

The best way to please your employer is to be kind, obedient, and pleasant to him, and to give him better service than anyone else in his office. In this way you can earn the highest position in the place, and then continue to develop your creative ability so that your employer will feel he would be blind without you. Perhaps your employer will then be glad to give you a partnership in the business.

Be sure to obey the reasonable commands of your boss or immediate superior. Try to keep him pleased by hard, intelligent, productive work, by extreme pleasantness and courtesy, and also by doing part of his work. Tolerate a cranky employer by increasing your kindness and courtesy, and internally ignoring his rash behavior. During meditation, concentrate at the point between the eyebrows and broadcast: "Father, calm my employer."

Perseverance, creative ability, attuning to the unlimited power of God in daily meditation, honest business methods, loyalty to your employer, thinking of the business you are employed in as your own business, tuning in with your immediate superior or the owner of the business and with your Cosmic Boss, God—by using these methods, you can unfailingly please both your office employer and your Divine Employer, God.

Remember, your real employer is God. He has employed you under someone to carry on His work. So, no matter how small your duty is, do it with the cheerful, careful consciousness of pleasing God. Anyone who works for God and respects all the employers under whom he has to work can never fail, but must succeed without limitation.

During meditation, say: "Father, bless me that I may be able to offer the best service in the business I am in. Father, bless me that I may please my employer and everyone I contact."

Service Should Be Your Goal

If you can convince your employer by your actions and creative ability that you can increase his income honestly, he will gladly give you the best position in the place for his own benefit. Your mind must be on creative ability and not on money making, and then money will be your slave instead of your master.

Most workers want high positions, but they forget to develop the necessary qualities of efficiency, creative ability, loyalty, and unselfish selfishness. To desire your own upliftment by making more money for the business you work for is not a sin, but is called "unselfish selfishness." Your "selfishness" must be directed toward the unselfish desire of helping your employer.

Remember that developing your usefulness is the surest way of attracting notice and success. No creative businessman can carry out his work by himself, and the largest and smallest concerns the world over are looking for honest, loyal, dependable, energetic, creative workers.

Develop Your Creative Ability

You must think creatively every day and equip yourself with the necessary knowledge and experience that your business demands. Creative thinking consists of going into the Silence every day for at least half an hour, and in putting your entire mind and concentration on discovering how you can improve your line of work and how you can become fit for a position of greater responsibility in your present business.

If there is a chance of promotion in the business you are in, continue using your creative ability for the wellbeing of your employer's business. But if your work is mechanical and has no future, develop your creative ability in a business that attracts you, and then secure a position in that business. When you are sure that you have a position in the business you like, then quit your former, get-by job.

If you develop your concentration and creative ability, you can learn to love any kind of work and can develop your efficiency and success in any direction you choose. But it is better to use your creative ability in work to which you are instinctively attracted, than in work to which you have to awaken your interest anew.

If you don't like to work for others, you must learn to be your own employer and employee. You must use your creative ability to acquire complete knowledge and experience in one branch of a very serviceable business. Use your creative concentration to gather capital for your business by working and borrowing; save money for it by leading a frugal life.

Congenital defects of a non-productive, non-intelligent mind can only be removed by meditation and creative thinking. Contact with God can remove all human limitations that impede success. Learn to receive success vibrations from God during meditation, and from successful men in the world.

The use of your creative ability will lead you to the sphere of unlimited success. By daily thinking about your line of work and the business you are in, and by business training and experience acquired in school or at work, you will find your knowledge of your business increasing a hundred-fold.

Acquired business experience must be expanded by constantly using common sense and creative ability. Penetrate deeply into the region of creative thought, and you will learn from A to Z about a business and will be able to manage any business in the best possible way. Use creative intelligence to cut down overhead expense and discover better methods of production, advertising, and distribution.

Selfishness in Business

Selfishness is the metaphysical blunder which leads self-seeking industries to undergo the throes of periodic depressions and false inflations.

If all the businessmen of the world are selfish, then each businessman has millions of inimical competitors. But, if each businessman wants to succeed by including the success of others in his success, then each businessman will have millions of helping business friends. "Each for all and all for each" must be the motto for real success and happiness in business.

Your Most Important Engagements

Systematize and schedule your engagements. Your business engagements are important, and for them you sacrifice your equally important engagements of daily physical exercise, and of bathing the nerves and mind with the peace of meditation. Your business engagements have always come first in your consideration. They can remain the most important until you are called away into the Mystery beyond. But I advocate evenness of development and prosperity. I do not believe in spiritual aspiration being chloroformed by business madness.

Many people think that unless one is "at it" day and night he is going to be left behind. That is not true. The one sided business-bent man, forgetful of the other duties of life, is not the truly successful man. It requires the greatest skill to live life evenly, rightly, and successfully. He who only keeps engagements with money is left behind by God.

Yet God talks to us very loudly through the pangs of hunger He has given us to remind us that we must make money to support our physical bodies.

Using all our mental powers to maintain our physical bodies should not be the goal of life. There is little difference between eating food from a gold plate or an ordinary plate—in both cases, the food satisfies hunger. Then why continue to multiply self-created, useless desires, and to work night and day in pursuit of things one does not need?

Your engagement with business is important, but your appointment with serving others is more important, and your engagement with meditation, God, and Truth is most important. Don't say that you are too busy with keeping the wolf from the door to have time for the development of heavenly qualities. Break your self-satisfied, immovable bad habit of idolizing your less important engagements and utterly ignoring your most important engagement with wisdom. No one else will answer for your actions, though others often keep you enmeshed in useless frivolities and so-called important engagements.

Engagements with Over-activity and Mr. Idleness both lead to misery. It is time for the modern man to shake his drowsiness of centuries and systematize his life. The modern man has learned to apply science, psychology, and system to his business for his material comfort. He ought also to apply system and science to improve his health, prosperity, wisdom, and social life. In order to do that, he must not give all his time to business, which only insures the hope of physical comfort.

People forget that living too luxuriously means a corresponding increase in use of nerve and brain energy, and the expenditure of longevity! Most people become so engrossed in making money that they cannot enjoy the comforts they have acquired.

How to Select Your Business Associates

The true success of any business depends upon the right business leader and his proper associates, and the right business management plus the right business environment. There are some businesses run by a single individual, but most businesses need to be run by a group of intelligent associates. When a business run by a single individual finds itself expanding, the owner may have to employ associates, but no matter whom you employ, always keep the controlling interest of your business in your own hands.

Most business concerns fail due to the lack of proper business associates. Employees should be judged by their previous record of success and their creative intelligence. Avoid silken-tongued but insincere, or impulsive, business associates. Such people will retard the progress of your business, if they do not entirely ruin it.

You must depend not only on references but also on keen observation, intelligence, open-mindedness, and intuition in order to select business associates with superior qualities. It is also a good idea to study the horoscope of a prospective business associate. If properly interpreted, the stars indicate an individual's good or evil habits of a former incarnation, which appear now as instincts and hereditary tendencies.

Tests of Character and Ability

Attracting honest, loyal, friendly, intelligent business associates, who will make your business their business and your ambition their ambition, is the best way to conduct a business. Look for creative ability, intelligence, and above all, trustworthiness in your business associates.

Don't take for granted the integrity of a business associate. Be sure to test him directly or indirectly, through friends or detectives. Give him a temptation and see how he reacts. Through friends, try to make your business associates talk against you, and find out what their intentions are. Forgive every minor fault twice or thrice, but never overlook treachery. A business associate who is treacherous toward you will repeat the same act when you are least expecting it, and can do you irreparable damage.

If a business associate is profligate, drinks too much, or shows no shame when criticized for his moral conduct, excuse him several times, giving him a chance to reform. If he fails to show signs of contriteness and improvement, discharge him.

Don't employ a slow-to-understand person, or a mentally or physically lazy person. A mentally lazy person grunts and moans, and considers it a terrible expenditure of energy to create, plan, or think about your business success.

Honesty and Loyalty in Business Relations

Do not keep a dishonest person in your employ. You can never tell what such a person might do to your business. Be sure to find out from his previous employer about his character, ability, and honesty. On the other hand, if you are an employee and you repeatedly hear something very negative about your prospective employer, then be sure to stay away from him altogether.

Never let a friend take advantage of you just because you are his friend. Business must be conducted strictly on business principles. Those business associates who stand by you in your troubles are your best friends. Never take into business a friend who would not take orders from you or follow your advice, due to wrong familiarity.

Read Character Through the Eyes

THE INTUITIVE WAY

The history of an individual is in his brain, and is reflected in the eyes, which show the character, habits, and the soul of an individual. Beware of shifting, untrustworthy eyes, cruel eyes, and crafty, sarcastic, revengeful eyes. Beware of hate-projecting eyes, and lack of straightforwardness in the eyes. If you feel an automatic, intuitive shrinking after looking fully in the eyes of an individual, then beware of that person.

The Spiritual Way

After deep meditation, hold your mind at the point between the eyebrows and visualize the eyes of your prospective employee or partner. Study the feeling in your heart. If you feel fear, don't employ such a person.

The First Impression

Keep your soul unprejudiced and look penetratingly into the eyes of the person you are interviewing, the first time you meet him. If you remain calm and receptive, your impression at first sight will be correct.

The Magnetic Way

After deep meditation, pray: "Father, send me my proper business associate through my spiritual magnetism, increased through Thy Grace."

CHAPTER 7

STORIES OF SUCCESS

A Saint's Wisdom

One day as I was starting on a pilgrimage, a saint said to me, "Do not ask for anything to eat from anyone, and do not accept money from anyone, not even from your father." I said, "But suppose I do not get anything to eat, and I starve to death?" He said, "Then die! Die to know that you live by the power of God, and not by bread."

Remember, we are all living directly by the power of God. When you know that, the whole world will be at your command. Claim your divinity first. Unite yourself with God. Receive your blessings from the hand of God first. Realize that all power, blessings, wealth, and health come from Him.

The Big Frog and the Little Frog

A big, fat frog and a little frog fell into a milk pail with tall, slippery sides. They swam and swam for hours trying to get out. Exhausted, the big frog moaned, "Little brother frog, I am giving up!" and he sank to the bottom of the pail.

The little frog thought to himself, "If I give up I will die, so I must keep on swimming." Two hours passed, and the little frog thought he could do no more. But as he thought of his dead brother frog, he roused his will, saying, "To give up is certain death. I will keep on paddling until I die, if death is to come, but I will not give up trying, for while there is life there is still hope."

Intoxicated with determination, the little frog kept on paddling. After hours, when he felt paralyzed with fatigue and could paddle no more, he suddenly felt a big lump under his feet. His incessant paddling had churned the milk into butter! Standing on the butter mound with great joy, the little frog leaped from the milk pail to freedom.

Remember, we are all in the slippery milk pail of life, trying to get free from our troubles like the two frogs. Most people give up trying and fail like the big frog. But we must learn to persevere in our effort toward one goal, as the little frog did. Then, we shall churn an opportunity by our God-guided, unflinching will power, and will be able to hop out of the milk pail of trials onto the safe ground of eternal success. By not giving up, we develop will power, and win in everything we undertake.

Victory Comes through the Correct Method

A young man came to me for help saying that, no matter what business venture he tried, he always failed. I said, "Go and meditate and say, 'Every day I am getting richer and richer.'" He tried to follow my instructions, but in about a month he came back and said, "It doesn't work. I am getting poorer and poorer."

I said to him, "Isn't it true that as you were affirming, in the background of your mind a little voice was always saying, 'You poor simpleton, you know that you are getting poorer every day'?" He said, "Yes."

I said to him very emphatically, "You must be deeply in earnest about what you are affirming. You must charge your mind with its importance, and you must continuously affirm it—this will greatly stimulate your will power. In addition, you must work out a step-by-step plan, as you are guided by divine law. Remember, it is your creative ability, your present congenial environment, and your good karma of the past that can bring you prosperity. If you take the divine law and use it, all other laws of bad karma and wrong environment will be destroyed."

I told the young man to meditate with me; when I knew that he felt the inner happiness of contact with the Divine,

I said, "Now it will work." Still he was doubtful and replied, "I do not believe it will work."

I said, "All right, in two weeks I am going to make $5,000 through you."

"$5,000 through me?!" he shouted.

I said, "Yes. Let us meditate and ask God how we should invest our money in order to make $5,000." We sat in meditation until the divine contact was made. When the contact came, I said, "Father, tell me what to do." During the meditation I saw two houses. We bought those two houses, and soon after, someone else wanted them and paid me $5,000 more than I had paid.

You must always be guided by divine power, which is unfailing. As I perceive, so may you perceive. As I behold, so may you behold the ethereal power that flows through you, through your speech, your brain, your body, your thoughts. Every thought is a channel through which the divine light is passing. Open your hearts that the Divine Flood may pass through you.

God's Blessing

In 1925 when I was beginning a lecture series in San Francisco, I found I had only $200 in the bank, with no other available funds in sight and a large institution to finance. When I told my secretary that I had only $200 in the bank, he nearly fell over. I said, "What is the matter with you?! God is with us. He won't leave us now. Within seven days He will give us all the money we need."

As I was walking in front of the Palace Hotel a few days later, a man came to me and said, "I would like to help you." I protested, "But you do not even know me." He replied, "I know you from your eyes," and at once wrote me a check for $27,000. This is the money I used to start the publication of Inner Culture magazine.

Two Blind Men Who Sought Riches

Akbar the Great was one of the greatest kings of India. He was called "Guardian of Mankind" because of the benevolence of his rule, and the devoted zeal with which he sought to regain lost sections of the once vast empire.

This charitable King showered good on needy individuals and social groups everywhere.

One day as the King's procession passed along the boulevard, he saw two blind men, sitting about twenty yards apart, shouting for alms. The King stopped his carriage to investigate. The first blind man was shouting, "To whom the King gives, he alone becomes rich." The second blind man was shouting, "To whom God gives, he alone becomes rich."

Whenever his procession drove along the boulevard, he heard these demands for riches from himself and from God. At last, the King, feeling flattered by the first blind man's utterance that "To whom the King gives, he alone becomes rich," ordered a large loaf of bread to be baked with the inside filled with solid gold. The King gave this loaf to the first blind man, and completely ignored the second blind man, who believed that God alone could make him rich.

After being away on a hunting trip for several weeks, the King again passed along the boulevard and came to the first blind man to whom he had given the loaf. This man was still shouting, "To whom the King gives, he alone becomes rich." The King asked, "What did you do with the loaf I gave you?" The blind man replied, "Your Royal Highness, the loaf you gave me was too large and heavy. I'm afraid it was not well baked, so I sold it to the other blind man for ten cents. I was happy to receive those ten cents."

The second blind man was no longer on the street. Upon inquiry, Akbar discovered that the second blind man had given the loaf to his wife, who had opened it and found the gold. With this she bought a home.

Upon learning this, the King, with inner humility but with outward wrath, rebuked the first blind man, saying, "You fool, you gave away my gold-stuffed loaf to your friend who depended upon God and not upon me for wealth. From now on you must change your motto and shout, like your friend, "To whom God gives, he alone becomes rich."

This story has a wonderful moral. Millions of people today think that all wealth comes from banks, factories, jobs, and through personal ability. This great depression* has proven that America is the most prosperous starving nation on the face of the globe. When the wealthiest country on earth, without any national catastrophe, can be suddenly thrown into poverty, it proves that there are divine laws which govern our physical, mental, spiritual, and financial lives.

---

* This article was written in 1934.

Every day strive to be healthy, wealthy, wise, and happy, not by taking away the health, wealth, and happiness of others, but by analyzing and planning everything you do, in order to make others better and happier while you are trying to become better and happier yourself. Learn to include the happiness and welfare of others in your own happiness.

Pray sincerely: "Father, bless us, that we may remember Thee always, and never forget that all things flow from Thee."

Making money honestly and industriously to serve God's work is the next greatest art after the art of realizing God.

To earn money abundantly, unselfishly, honestly, and quickly, for God and God's work and to make others happy, helps develop many sterling character qualities that will aid you on the spiritual as well as the material path.

With blessings
Paramhansa Yogananda
Encinitas - April 3rd 1951
4 P.M.

Chapter 8

"Seek Ye First the Kingdom of God"

Most people reason that if they first have prosperity, then they can think of God. But you must have God first. If you once have that great contact with God, then the prosperity of the universe will be at your feet. Don't forget that God is your provider.

No matter what your faults are, when your whole consciousness is directed toward God, toward the Silence, then you are with God. When you perform all the duties of life cheerfully, without letting anything upset you, then you have spiritual happiness.

You are living directly by the power of God. Suppose God suddenly changed the climate of this country. How would you live? Where would you find food? Remember that God is the sustainer of the life He has given you. Even though He made that life dependent upon food, still He is the direct support. He is the Cause of everything, so when you lose your connection with God you are bound to suffer.

Yogis have learned that God can never be found outside themselves, but when you go deep within your soul, into the temple of God, you can say, "No one in the whole world cares for my health, prosperity, and happiness as my Father does. He is with me always."

No more shall you depend upon man for prosperity, for God is the source of prosperity, health, power, and immortality. The yogi says, "Be free within. Know God as your provider and don't live in poverty consciousness."

Real prosperity is attained when you realize that God is your provider and that you are absolutely dependent upon Him. When you have that consciousness, you don't care what happens because you are in the immortal arms of God. Jesus had no money, and yet he was the happiest person in the world. He had God, and he knew that God was his provider.

You are paralyzing your faculty for success by thoughts of fear. Success and perfection of mind and body are man's inherent qualities because he is made in God's image. In order to be able to claim his birthright, however, he must first rid himself of the delusion of his own limitations.

God owns everything. Therefore, know at all times that as God's child, you own everything that belongs to the Father. You must feel fully satisfied and contented, knowing you have access to all your Father's possessions. Your native endowment is perfection and prosperity, but you choose to be imperfect and poor. The sense of possessing everything must be a mental habit with each individual.

The surest way to all-round efficiency, or to the attainment of health, wealth, peace, and wisdom, lies in broadcasting your desires to God through your calm mental microphone until you receive His answer in the form of fulfillment of your proper desires. You must always remember, however, that God helps those who help themselves, so you must put forth every effort for accomplishment.

Visualizations or affirmations of success may strengthen your subconscious mind, which in turn encourages your conscious mind. However, the conscious mind still has to *achieve* the success and is hindered by the law of cause and effect. The conscious mind cannot change your karma in order to bring positive success. But when the human mind can contact God, then the superconscious mind can be sure of success, due to the unlimited power of God.

Think of Divine Abundance as a mighty refreshing rain—whatever receptacle you have at hand will receive it. If you hold up a tin cup, you will receive only a cupful. If you hold up a barrel, that will be filled. What kind of a receptacle are you holding up to Divine Abundance? Perhaps your receptacle is defective. If so, it must be repaired by casting out all fear, hate, doubt, and envy, and then be cleansed by the purifying waters of peace, tranquility, devotion, and love.

Divine Abundance follows the law of service and generosity. Give and then receive. Give to the world the best you have, and the best will come back to you.

All prosperity is measured out to man according to the law of cause and effect from this life and all past lives. This explains why some are born poor or unhealthy, and others healthy and wealthy. Men were originally sons of God made in His image with free choice and equal powers of accomplishment. Through the misuse of his God-given reason and will power, man became controlled by the law of action (karma) and thus limited his life. A man's success depends not only upon his intelligence and efficiency, but also upon the nature of his past actions. However, there is a way to overcome the unfavorable results of past actions. They must be destroyed and a new direction set in motion.

Some psychologists erroneously teach that by visualizing Henry Ford, one can become like Henry Ford. No matter how strongly all the people in the world visualize Henry Ford, all of them could not become like him. This is impossible according to the law of karma, which governs this earth and the destinies of men.

Not all the people of the earth can become millionaires, but all people by real effort can regain their lost divinity and become sons of God.

The surest way to prosperity lies, not in begging through wrong prayer, but in establishing first your oneness with God, and afterward demanding the divine son's share. That is why Jesus said that men of the world wrongly seek bread first, but that they should seek first the Kingdom of God, then all things, all prosperity, will be added, unasked for, unto them.

This is easier said than done. You must learn to demonstrate this truth in your life. You must remember that Jesus spoke from experience when he said, "I and my Father are One." Thus He could command the storms to stop, turn water into wine, and heal the physically and mentally suffering. He was spiritually successful, and hence knew the art of mental and physical success.

The man of powerful concentration must ask God to direct his focused mind to the right place for right success. Passive people want God to do all the work, and egotists ascribe all their success to themselves. Passive people do not use the power of God's intelligence within them. Egotists, though using God-given intelligence, forget to ask God's direction as to where the intelligence should be used.

You must avoid both passivity and egotism. In the early morning and before going to bed, you must make positive contact with God in order to succeed.

Try to harmonize the dollar craving with the spiritual craving. Let neither rule the other. Don't be so busy feeding the flesh that you find no time for meditation or spiritual service. On the other hand, don't think you are too spiritual to wish for material success. One who is unsuccessful in the material life cannot enter Heaven. The spiritually selfish man, ignoring material life, is punished with a loss of mental balance. All material work should be service to your fellow beings.

Don't be one sided. Lead a scheduled life and priori-tize your duties. (Duties should be done with pleasure and a sense of privilege, not with the feeling of paying a debt.) Consciousness of spiritual and moral duty should reign in your mind predominantly, above all other duties. Intellectual duty is superior to material duty. Material duty is very important and must be supplemented with social, patriotic, and international duties.

Your soul's message cannot reach God through your mental microphone if it is broken by hammers of restless-ness, so you must repair it by practicing deep silence both in the morning and before sleep, until all restless thoughts disappear. When the mental microphone is repaired by calmness, affirm deeply: "My Father and I are One," until you feel the response of God through ever-increasing peace in meditation. This increasing peace, or bliss, is the surest proof of God's contact and response.

You must broadcast your message, "My Father and I are One," until you feel the overpowering, all-solacing bliss of God. When this happens, you have made the contact. Then demand your celestial right by affirming, "Father, I am Thy child. Guide me to my right prosperity."

Do not will and act first, but contact God first and thus harness your will and activity to the right goal.

You cannot get an answer by simply calling to someone through a microphone and then running away. So, also, you must not pray once and run away, but you must continuously broadcast your prayer to God through your calm mental microphone until you hear His voice. Most people do not pray with the determination to receive a response.

The surest way to the attainment of health, wealth, peace, and wisdom, lies in first reclaiming your lost divinity by continuously broadcasting your message to God through your calm mental microphone until you receive His answer through the increased bliss of meditation.

Take a spiritual or material desire and float it in the Cosmic Vibration, which you can hear and feel in the practice of the AUM technique* of meditation. Desire is realized when you are in conscious contact with the Cosmic Vibration. Try to have one desire above all—to contact God always, in everything. Share this supreme desire again and again with the Cosmic Vibration. Having Him, you will have everything.

Affirm daily: "Lord, Thou art my provider. Manifest Thy prosperity through me. Father, Thou art my riches; I am rich. Thou art the owner of all things. I am Thy child. I have what Thou hast." Affirm this in the morning before going to work. Remember to live by God's laws, and He will show you the way.

Riches of the world are perishable, but the riches of God are imperishable. Through millions of incarnations, you have tortured your soul; the only way to find release is to find God. Having Him you will find deeper joy than

---

* For information on this meditation technique, contact the publisher.

from all the riches in the world. Be a child of the Father of the Universe and say: "Earthly riches are but toys. I am rich, for I have my God." Be sure of Him first, and everlasting riches will be yours in this life and beyond.

Index

abundance, 26, 115, 119–21, 124, 125

action
    past affecting, 45–47, 98, 99
    will power and, 54
    See also karma

affirmations, 62, 117, 118, 125, 131

Association, power of, 87–89

attention
    desires and, 37
    failure and, 51
    focusing, 15, 17, 18, 20, 23
    on work, 64
    See also concentration

Attraction, power of, 84, 88

AUM meditation, 51, 130, 131

The Big Frog and the Little Frog, 115–16

brain, 18, 52

business
    creativity in, 103–5
    dishonesty in, 110
    employee qualities in, 109, 110

employer relationship and, 100–101
    prayer for, 102, 112
    self-employed in, 104, 108
    selfishness in, 105–6
    treachery in, 110
    unselfish selfishness in, 103
    See also vocation

calmness
    prayer and, 26
    problems and, 16

character insights, 111, 112

Child of God, 68. *See also* Sons of God

children, 40, 41

concentration
    desires and, 73
    magnetism and, 86
    meditation and, 49, 50
    power of, 48, 73–75, 128
    success and, 73, 74
    See also attention

Cosmic magnetism, 88

Cosmic Plan, 97
Cosmic Vibration, 130, 131
creativity, 103–5

death
 fear and, 56, 57
 God and, 115
 will power and, 77
desires
 attention and, 37
 concentration and, 73
 defined, 77
 Divine Magnetic Power and, 90
 eliminating, 49
 Heart's, 96, 97
 meditation and, 125
 unnecessary, 35–37
 See also needs
destiny, 17, 25
determination
 *The Big Frog and the Little
  Frog* and, 115, 116
 effects of, 30, 46, 47
 happiness and, 29

 inferiority complex and, 52
 of mind, 40
 prayer and, 130
 success and, 99
 vocation and, 40, 95
 will power and, 75, 76
diet, 85
disease
 cause of, 55, 56
 eliminating, 51, 52
dishonesty, 110
Divine Abundance, 126
Divine Love, 22
Divine Magnetic Power, 90
Divine Will
 attunement with, 26, 30, 80
 meditation and, 25, 82
 realized man and, 78
 success and, 24, 25
 See also will power

egotism, 128
employee qualities, 109, 110
employer. *See* business

Energization Exercises, 51, 86
energy
    life, 18
    magnetism and, 87
    scattering, 17, 87
    of will power, 19

failure
    attention and, 51
    fear of, 48
    habits and, 63, 73
    of plans, 15
    refusing, 17, 18, 20, 50, 95
    seeds of, 45, 46, 50
    and success, 75
fasting, 86
fear
    death and, 56, 57
    effect of, 19, 53
    of failure, 48
    germination of, 54
    mind and, 53–55
    success and, 19, 20
    thoughts of, 124

    uprooting, 55
    will power and, 19, 48, 53
fearlessness, 55, 56
finances, 46–48, 74. *See also*
    money; prosperity
First Impression technique,
    112
Ford, Henry, 46, 127
freedom, 23, 29

God
    abundance and, 26, 124, 125
    death and, 56, 57, 115
    faith in, 52, 119–21
    loving, 81
    meditation and, 81, 129
    power from, 15, 28, 123
    prayer to, 81
    prosperity and, 123, 124, 127,
        130
    serving, 122
    sons of, 68, 82, 126, 127
    voice of, 24
    will power and, 81

God's Blessing, 119

habits
  bad, 23, 24
  defined, 61
  failure and, 63, 73
  good, 24
  life and, 63
  material, 23
  mental, 23, 61–63, 73
  success and, 63
  will power and, 63
handshake, 89, 90
happiness
  determination and, 29
  in life, 28
  money and, 39
  true, 37
healing, 79
heart's desire, 96, 97
Hon Sau technique, 51, 52
horoscope, 109

indifference attitude, 78

inferiority complex, 52
inner Self, 16, 24, 30, 31
Intuitive Way technique, 111

Jesus, 25, 80, 99, 124, 127

karma
  burning, 51
  effects of, 126, 127
  serving others and, 22, 49, 69
  success and, 125
  See also action; seeds of karma
kingdom of Success, 65

law of Prosperity, 93
law of Success, 65, 69
law of Unselfishness, 90, 93
laws of nature, 23, 75
life
  balance in, 67, 128, 129
  children and, 40, 41
  as a dream, 81
  fulfillment of, 20
  habits and, 63

happiness in, 28
opportunity in, 15, 66
purpose in, 21, 28, 35, 37–39, 74
See also past lives;
　　reincarnation
love, Divine, 22

agnetic Way technique, 112
magnetism
　cosmic, 88
　defined, 83
　Divine, 90
　energy and, 87
　mental, 86
　power of association and,
　　87–89
　power of attraction and, 84, 88
meditation
　AUM, 51, 130, 131
　concentration and, 49, 50
　desires and, 125
　Divine Will and, 25, 82
　magnetism and, 83
　success and, 104, 105

unity with God and, 81, 129
value of, 27, 49, 50
will power and, 79
meetings, 106, 107
mental
　habits, 23, 61–63, 73
　magnetism, 86
mind
　creativity and, 103
　determination of, 40
　fear and, 53–55
　happiness of, 29
　karma and, 125
　life energy and, 18
　self-analysis and, 21
　strength of, 39
　Universal, 26
　will power, 17
　See also mental
money, 39, 68, 122. *See also*
　finances; prosperity

natural ability, 15
Nature, laws of, 23, 75

needs, 35–38. *See also* desires

opportunity in life, 15, 66

Paramhansa Yogananda, 99, 100
past lives
    affecting action, 45–47, 98,
        99
    affecting success, 21, 46, 47,
        126, 127, 131, 132
    disease and, 55, 56
    prosperity and, 69, 126
    See also reincarnation
patience, 62, 65
peace, 39, 40, 74
perseverance, 46, 77. *See also*
    determination
power, 15, 30
power of association, 87–89
power of attraction, 84, 88
power of concentration, 48,
    73–75, 128
prayer
    for business, 102, 112

    determination and, 130
    to God, 81, 122
    for success, 61, 131
    for will power, 82–83
problems, 16, 73
prosperity
    God source of, 123, 124, 127,
        130
    law of, 93
    law of unselfishness and, 90
    past action and, 69, 126
    See also finances; money

realized man, 78
reincarnation
    affecting action, 45–47
    affecting success, 126, 127,
        131, 132
    disease and, 55–56
    seed tendencies and, 54
    See also past lives
responsibility, 22

A Saint's Wisdom, 115

salvation, 22
seeds of karma
   burning, 51, 56
   of failure, 45, 46, 50
   tendencies, 54
self-analysis, 21, 22, 24, 96
self-control. *See* habits
self-employed, 104, 108
self-improvement, 39
selfishness, 105, 106
self-mastery, 23
self-punishment, 29
senses, 37
service to others, 22, 49, 67–69,
       97–98, 126
sex, 85
Sons of God, 68, 82, 126, 127
Spiritual Way technique, 111–12
stories, success
   *The Big Frog and the Little
       Frog,* 115–16
   God's Blessing, 119
   A Saint's Wisdom, 115
   Two Blind Men Who Sought

   Riches, 119–21
   *Victory Comes through the
       Correct Method,* 117–18
success
   concentration and, 73, 74
   determination and, 99
   Divine Will and, 24, 25
   failure and, 75
   fear and, 19, 20
   habits and, 63
   Kingdom of, 65
   law of, 65, 69
   meditation and, 104, 105
   needs and, 36, 37
   past lives affecting, 21, 46,
       47, 126, 127, 131, 132
   prayer for, 61, 131
   stages of, 65
   will power and, 16, 17
Success, Law of, 65
Supreme Will. *See* Divine Will

thoughts
   of fear, 124

habitual, 16, 23, 61–63
negative, 62, 63
positive, 16
strength of, 15
treachery, 110
trials, 98, 99
*Two Blind Men Who Sought
    Riches*, 119–21

universal Mind, 26
unselfish selfishness, 103
unselfishness, Law of, 90

vibration, 16
*Victory Comes through the
    Correct Method*, 117–18
visualization, 125
vocation
    determination in, 40, 95
    effort in, 94
    heart's desire in, 96, 97
    progressing in, 64–65
    service in, 93
    temporary, 94
    See also business

volition. *See* will power

will power
    action and, 54
    *The Big Frog and the Little
        Frog* and, 115, 116
    constructive, 18
    death and, 77
    determination and, 75, 76
    Divine Will and, 25, 26, 30,
        80, 82
    dynamic/conscious, 16–19,
        48, 54, 75
    energy of, 19
    fear and, 19, 48, 53
    God and, 81
    habits and, 63
    healing with, 79
    mechanical, 16
    meditation and, 79
    nature supporting, 75
    persevering, 46, 77
    prayer for, 82–83
    success and, 16, 17

See also determination
workplace. *See* vocation

yogi, 50, 79–80, 123, 124

List of Illustrations

1. Yogananda with companions at the Taj Mahal. 13

2. Yogananda, the Palace of Fine Arts in San Francisco. . 33

3. Yogananda with a group of the delegates of the International Congress of Religious Liberals at Boston, MA, 1920 43

4. Yogananda in Yosemite National Park 59

5. Yogananda wearing "business suit," 1940's 71

6. Free Lectures Poster for Yogananda's United States lecture series in the 1920-30's. 91

7. Yogananda with President Coolidge, at the White House 113

8. Meditating on the beach at Encinitas, CA. 123

9. Yogananda with squirrel in San Francisco. 134

Paramhansa Yogananda was the first yoga master of India to permanently live and teach in the West. Yogananda arrived in America in 1920, and traveled throughout the United States on what he called his 'spiritual campaigns'. His enthusiastic audiences filled the largest halls in America. A national sensation, Yogananda's lectures and books were extensively written about by the major media of the era, including *Time Magazine*, *Newsweek*, and *Life*. He was even invited to the White House by President Calvin Coolidge. Yogananda continued to lecture and write up to his passing in 1952.

As the author of ***Autobiography of a Yogi***, first published in 1946, Yogananda helped launch a spiritual revolution throughout the world. His message was nonsectarian and universal.

FURTHER EXPLORATIONS

If you are inspired by *How to Be a Success* and would like to learn more about Paramhansa Yogananda and his teachings, Crystal Clarity Publishers offers many additional resources to assist you. The following is a partial list of titles that may interest you.

The Wisdom of Yogananda Series

The **Wisdom of Yogananda Series** features writings of Paramhansa Yogananda not available elsewhere. These books express the Master's expansive and compassionate wisdom, his sense of fun, and his practical spiritual guidance. The books include writings from his earliest years in America, in an approachable, easy-to-read format. The words of the Master are presented with minimal editing, to capture the fresh and original voice of one of the most highly regarded spiritual teachers of the 20th Century.

How to Be Happy All the Time
The Wisdom of Yogananda Series, Volume 1
Paramhansa Yogananda

The human drive for happiness is one of our most far-reaching and fundamental needs. Yet, despite our desperate search for happiness, according to a recent Gallup Poll, only a minority of North Americans describe themselves as "very happy." It seems that very few of us have truly unlocked the secrets of lasting joy and inner peace.

In this volume of new, not available elsewhere, Paramhansa Yogananda, playfully and powerfully explains virtually everything needed to lead a happier, more fulfilling life. Topics covered include: looking for happiness in the right places; choosing to be happy; tools and techniques for achieving happiness; sharing happiness with others; balancing success and happiness, and many more.

Karma and Reincarnation
The Wisdom of Yogananda Series, Volume 2
Paramhansa Yogananda

The interrelated ideas of karma and reincarnation have intrigued us for millennia. The idea of "karma" has become mainstream while belief in reincarnation is now at an all-time high in the West. Yet, for all of the burgeoning interest, very few of us truly understand what these terms mean and how these principles work.

In this book Yogananda definitively reveals the truth behind karma, death, reincarnation, and the afterlife. With clarity and simplicity, Yogananda makes the mysterious understandable. Topics covered include: how karma works; how we can change our karma; the relationship between karma and reincarnation; what we can learn from our past lives; how to overcome karmic obstacles; how to die with uplifted consciousness; what happens after death; the true purpose of life, and much more.

Spiritual Relationships
The Wisdom of Yogananda Series, Volume 3
Paramhansa Yogananda

Discover how to express your own highest potential in relationships of friendship, love, marriage, and family. Warmly, realistically, with humor and humanity, Yogananda shows you the folly of selfishness and the practical steps toward expansive love for others.

Learn to experience more harmony in your life. Friendship, love, marriage, and children can offer us our greatest joys in life or our greatest sorrows. Selfless love is the essential key to happiness in all our relationships, but how do we practice it?

In this book Yogananda shares fresh inspiration and practical guidance on: friendship—broadening your sympathies and expanding the boundaries of your love; how to cure bad habits that spell the death of true friendship—judgement, jealousy, over-sensitivity, unkindness, and more; how to choose the right partner and create a lasting marriage; sex in marriage and how to conceive a spiritual child; problems that arise in marriage and what to do about them; the divine plan uniting parents and children; the Universal Love behind all your relationships.

Other titles on Material & Business Success

Swami Kriyananda, direct disciple of Yogananda, has published several best-selling books on business topics such as leadership and money. He has also written a home-study course on success using yogic principles.

Material Success Through Yoga Principles
A Twenty-Six Lesson, Study-at-Home Course
Swami Kriyananda (J. Donald Walters)

These lessons compellingly communicate that spirituality and material success are not separate, unrelated aspects of life. These two fields of endeavor can indeed help each other. By following yoga principles, you can have all the benefits of true success: happiness, inner peace, understanding, true friendships, and life's normal comforts without the suffocation of meaningless luxury.

Each of the twenty-six lessons is packed with information, examples, stories, inspiration, and solutions to common problems that face every person seeking success. By applying the principles and practices taught in this course, business, government, and educational leaders will be better prepared to guide our future directions with dignity, right-action, and success. It is also of immense help to the millions who suffer from symptoms of stressful business rhythms, and who seek a more balanced approach to personal satisfaction through their work.

"[This] is a significant contribution to the transformation of human awareness. . . . [and] provides the platform on which ethics and practicality meet, each strengthening the other. I sincerely recommend that business and government leaders who want to be morally, psychologically, and practically prepared for the challenges that face our world study this course and apply its lessons with all due urgency, making it part of their training program for leaders of tomorrow."

— Professor Ervin Laszlo, Nobel Peace Prize Nominee, Founder and President, Club of Budapest

"I knew I had tapped into teachings that were very relevant and immediately applicable to my work as a manager in a large government agency. I read each lesson at home, and then brought the handy booklet with me to work and kept it on my desk for reference and to remind me of the key points in that lesson. I could reflect on these while at work and feel immediately inspired and recharged."

— Russ Reece, Director, Corporate Planning Bureau, California Franchise Tax Board

"As a project manager for a big engineering project, I am applying the principles of 'non-attachment' and 'people are more important than things' and finding that they are giving me amazing results. The feeling of joy that I experience throughout my day whether it be during meetings or even in heated discussions is directly due to the training I have received in this course."

— Arnab Chatterjee, Project Manager, IT Department, Boeing Corporation

The Art of Supportive Leadership
A Practical Guide for People in Positions of Responsibility
J. Donald Walters

Here is a new approach, one that views leadership in terms of shared accomplishment rather than personal advancement. Drawn from timeless Eastern wisdom, this book is clear, concise, and practical—designed from the start to quickly produce results even for those who don't have huge amounts of time to spare.

Used in training seminars in the U.S., Europe, and India, this book gives practical advice for leaders and emerging leaders to help them increase effectiveness, creativity, and team building. Individual entrepreneurs, corporations such as Kellogg, military and police personnel, and nonprofit organizations are using this approach.

"We've been looking for something like this for a long time. We use it in our Managers Training Workshop. This book is very practical, very readable, and concise. Highly recommended!"

— Kellogg Corporation

"The most depth and understanding of what a manager faces of the many management books I've read over the years. I plan to keep it on my desk as a daily reference."

— Ray Narragon, Sun Microsystems

Money Magnetism
How to Attract What You Need When You Need It
J. Donald Walters

This book can change your life by changing how you think and feel about money. According to the author, anyone can attract wealth: "There need be no limits to the flow of your abundance." Through numerous stories and examples from his own life and others', Swami Kriyananda vividly—sometimes humorously—shows you how and why the principles of money magnetism work, and how you can immediately start applying them to achieve greater success in your material and your spiritual life.

"A thoughtful, spiritual guide to financial and personal prosperity. This book has timeless wisdom and practical solutions."

— Maria Nemeth, author of *The Energy of Money*

"Money Magnetism *will help you take charge of your life. True abundance–of both the material and spiritual kind–can be found through the wisdom of this small but powerful book."*

— John Ernst, Richland Financial Services

"[This] is a very fine book. I thoroughly agree with it."

— Richard Russell, Dow Theory Letters

Other titles by Paramhansa Yogananda

Paramhansa Yogananda's best-known and most widely beloved book is *Autobiography of a Yogi*. This book has sold millions of copies worldwide and is considered one of the masterpieces of 20th Century spiritual literature. It is considered a must-read for sincere seekers of all paths.

Autobiography of a Yogi
Original 1946 Edition
Paramhansa Yogananda

Yogananda's *Autobiography* has entered the homes and hearts of millions of people all over the world. Reading it, one feels hope and finds peace. Many readers have given it to their friends and families, who in turn have given it to others. This Crystal Clarity publication is a verbatim reprinting of the original 1946 edition. Subsequent editions reflect revisions made after the author's death. The few thousand originals have long ago disappeared into the hands of collectors. Now it is possible to read the first edition, with all its inherent power, just as the great master originally intended it.

"In the original edition, published during Yogananda's life, one is more in contact with Yogananda himself. While Yogananda founded centers and organizations, his concern was more with guiding individuals to direct communion with Divinity rather than

with promoting any one church as opposed to another. This spirit is easier to grasp in the original edition of this great spiritual and yogic classic."

— David Frawley, Director, American Institute of Vedic Studies

Autobiography of a Yogi – Audio Book
Unabridged Edition
by Paramhansa Yogananda, read by Swami Kriyananda

This is a new unabridged recording of the original, 1946 unedited edition of *Autobiography of a Yogi*, presented on 16 CDs. Read by Swami Kriyananda, this is the only audio edition that is read by one of Yogananda's direct disciples—someone who both knew him and was directly trained by him.

Autobiography of a Yogi – Card Deck
52 Cards plus Booklet
Paramhansa Yogananda

Now for the first time, Paramhansa Yogananda's thrilling autobiography comes to new life in this beautiful full-color card deck and booklet. Each of the 52 cards features an inspiring quotation taken from the text of the Original 1946 First Edition—the preferred edition for both enthusiasts and collectors. The flip-side of each card features a photograph from the book, including previously unreleased and rare photographs of Yogananda. For the first time, these famous images and quotations will be portable, ensuring their use by the great Master's followers in their homes, altars, journals, autos, and purses. The enclosed booklet includes a history of the book, additional information about the quotations and photographs, and a user's guide for the card deck.

The Essence of the Bhagavad Gita
As Explained by Paramhansa Yogananda
As Remembered by His Disciple, Swami Kriyananda

Rarely in a lifetime does a new spiritual classic appear that has the power to change people's lives and transform future generations. This is such a book. *The Essence of the Bhagavad Gita Explained by Paramhansa Yogananda* shares the profound insights of Paramhansa Yogananda, as remembered by one of his few remaining direct disciples, Swami Kriyananda.

This revelation of India's best-loved scripture approaches it from an entirely fresh perspective, showing its deep allegorical meaning and also its down-to-earth practicality. The themes presented are universal: how to achieve victory in life in union with the divine; how to prepare for life's "final exam," death, and what happens afterward; how to triumph over all pain and suffering.

Swami Kriyananda worked with Paramhansa Yogananda in 1950 while the Master completed his commentary. At that time Yogananda commissioned him to disseminate his teachings worldwide. Kriyananda declares, "Yogananda's insights into the Gita are the most amazing, thrilling, and helpful of any I have ever read."

"It is doubtful that there has been a more important spiritual writing in the last 50 years than this soul-stirring, monumental work. What a gift! What a treasure!"

— Neale Donald Walsch, author of *Conversations with God*

Revelations of Christ
Proclaimed by Paramhansa Yogananda
Presented by his disciple, Swami Kriyananda

For years, our faith has been severely shaken by a growing series of attacks, including: the breakdown of church authority, the repeated discovery of ancient texts that supposedly contradict long-held beliefs, and the sometimes outlandish historical analyses of Scripture by academics. Together, these forces have helped create a substantial confusion and uncertainty about the true teachings and meaning of Christ's life. The rising tide of alternative beliefs proves that now, more than ever, people are yearning for a clear-minded, convincing, yet uplifting understanding of the life and teachings of Jesus Christ.

This galvanizing book, presenting the teachings of Christ from the experience and perspective of Paramhansa Yogananda, one of the greatest spiritual masters of the Twentieth Century, finally offers the fresh perspective on Christ's teachings for which the world has been waiting. This book presents us with an opportunity to understand and apply the Scriptures in a more reliable way than any other: by studying under those saints who have communed directly, in deep ecstasy, with Christ and God.

"Kriyananda's revelatory book gives us the enlightened, timeless wisdom of Jesus the Christ in a way that addresses the challenges of Twenty-first Century living."

— Michael Beckwith, Founder and Spiritual Director, Agape International Spiritual Center, author of *Inspirations of the Heart*

The Rubaiyat of Omar Khayyam
Explained by Paramhansa Yogananda
Edited by Swami Kriyananda

Omar Khayyam's famous poem, *The Rubaiyat,* is loved by Westerners as a hymn of praise to sensual delights. In the East, his quatrains enjoy a very different reputation — they are known as a deep allegory of the soul's romance with God. Now after more than eight centuries, Paramhansa Yogananda, one of the great yoga and spiritual teachers of our time, explains the mystery behind the sage and mystic's famous poem. This book contains the essence of that great revelation, edited by one of Yogananda's close direct disciples and best-selling author Swami Kriyananda.

"The most enchanting reading experience I've had in a decade."

— Wayne Dyer, author of *The Power of Intention*

There are several collections of the sayings, stories, and wisdom of Yogananda, each covering a diverse range of spiritual practices and topics, presented in an enjoyable, easy-to-read format.

Conversations with Yogananda
Edited with commentary by Swami Kriyananda

This is an unparalleled, first-hand account of the teachings of Paramhansa Yogananda. Featuring nearly 500 never-before-released stories, sayings, and insights, this is an extensive, yet eminently accessible, treasure trove of wisdom from one of the 20th Century's most famous yoga masters. Compiled and edited with commentary, by Swami Kriyananda, one of Yogananda's closest direct disciples.

The Essence of Self-Realization
Recorded, Compiled, and Edited by Swami Kriyananda

A fantastic volume of the stories, sayings, advice and wisdom of Paramhansa Yogananda, this book covers more than 20 essential topics about the spiritual path and practices. Subjects covered include: the true purpose of life, the folly of materialism, the essential unity of all religions, the laws of karma and reincarnation, grace vs. Self-effort, the need for a guru, how to pray effectively, meditation, and many more.

Other related titles

Yogananda has many direct disciples, individuals whom he personally trained to carry on various aspects of his mission after his passing. One of the best known of these disciples is Swami Kriyananda, the founder of Ananda and Crystal Clarity Publishers. Kriyananda's autobiography contains hundreds of stories about Yogananda, culled from the nearly four years that Kriyananda lived with and was trained by Yogananda. It offers the unique perspective of a disciple reflecting on his time with a great Master.

The Path—My Life with Paramhansa Yogananda
One Man's Search on the Only Path There Is
Swami Kriyananda (J. Donald Walters)

The Path is the moving story of Kriyananda's years with Paramhansa Yogananda. *The Path* completes Yogananda's life story and includes more than 400 never-before-published stories about Yogananda, India's emissary to the West and the first yoga master to spend the greater part of his life in America.

"Perfectly captures the personality of Paramhansa Yogananda. I am delighted that my brother disciple has produced this monumental work. I highly recommend The Path.*"*

— Roy Eugene Davis, Founder, Center for Spiritual Awareness

God Is for Everyone
Inspired by Paramhansa Yogananda
Written by Swami Kriyananda

This book outlines the core of Yogananda's teachings. *God Is for Everyone* presents a concept of God and spiritual meaning that will broadly appeal to everyone, from the most uncertain agnostic to the most fervent believer. Clearly and simply written, thoroughly non-sectarian and non-dogmatic in its approach, with a strong emphasis on the underlying unity of all religions, this is the perfect introduction to the spiritual path.

If you would like to learn how to begin your own practice of yoga postures, meditation, Kriya Yoga, and more, as taught by Yogananda and Kriyananda, we recommend the following titles.

Meditation for Starters
Swami Kriyananda

Meditation brings balance into our lives, providing an oasis of profound rest and renewal. Doctors are prescribing it for a variety of stress-related diseases. This award-winning book offers simple but powerful guidelines for attaining inner peace. Learn to prepare the body and mind for meditation with special breathing techniques and ways to focus and "let go"; develop superconscious awareness;

strengthen your willpower; improve your intuition and increase your calmness.

"*Meditation for Starters is one of the best introductions to meditation for the beginner.*"

— *Yoga + Joyful Living* magazine

"*A gentle guide to entering the most majestic, fulfilling dimensions of consciousness. Walters is a wise teacher whose words convey love and compassion. Read and listen and allow your life to change.*"

— Larry Dossey, M.D., author of *Prayer Is Good Medicine*

Awaken to Superconsciousness
How to Use Meditation for Inner Peace,
Intuitive Guidance, and Greater Awareness
Swami Kriyananda

Many people have experienced moments of raised consciousness and enlightenment — or 'Superconsciousness' — but do not know how to purposely enter such an exalted state. Superconsciousness is the hidden mechanism at work behind intuition, spiritual and physical healing, successful problem solving, and finding deep, lasting joy.

Through meditation, chanting, affirmation, and prayer, readers will learn how to reach this state successfully and regularly and how to maximize its beneficial effects. *Awaken to Superconsciousness* provides a comprehensive, easy-to-understand routine to help people tap into their wellspring of creativity, unlock intuitive guidance, and hear the silent voice of their soul.

Music for Inspiration

Crystal Clarity also makes available many music and audiobook resources. Here are some that you might find helpful to increase your energy or to create an atmosphere of peace and inspiration for your office.

Power Chants
Ananda Kirtan

Unlock your divine strength and energy. Chanting is an ancient technique for focusing and uplifting the mind and soul into higher states of consciousness. This recording will help you tap into the positive aspects of Power: the ability to strengthen and direct our will, creative energy, and inner resources toward the Divine, and to use our Power to control our spiritual destiny.

"Perfect for reaching higher states of consciousness, prayer, and lifting the spirits."
— Music Design

Relax: Meditations for Flute and Cello
With David Eby and Sharon Brooks
Music by Donald Walters

Experience tranquility and inner peace. Much more than just beautiful background music, this CD takes you on a journey deep within, helping you to experience a dynamic sense of peace and calmness. *Relax* is specifically designed to slow respiration and heart rate, bringing you to your calm center. The recording features fifteen melodies on flute and cello, accompanied by harp, guitar, keyboard, and strings.

David Eby, cellist for internationally renowned group Pink Martini, joins the highly acclaimed flutist, Sharon Brooks, for their second collaboration together. In addition to giving concerts together throughout the U.S. and abroad, they are both highly popular recording and performing artists.

AUM: Mantra of Eternity
Swami Kriyananda

This recording features nearly 70 minutes of continuous vocal chanting of AUM, the Sanskrit word meaning peace and oneness of spirit. AUM, the cosmic creative vibration, is extensively discussed by Yogananda in his book, *Autobiography of a Yogi*. Chanted here by his direct disciple, Swami Kriyananda, this recording is a stirring way to tune into this cosmic power.

Crystal Clarity Publishers

Crystal Clarity Publishers is recognized worldwide for its best-selling, original, unaltered edition of Paramhansa Yogananda's classic *Autobiography of a Yogi.* They also offer many additional resources to assist you in your spiritual journey including over ninety books, a wide variety of inspirational and relaxation music composed by Swami Kriyananda, Yogananda's direct disciple, and yoga and meditation DVDs.

For our online catalog, complete with secure ordering, please visit us on the web at:

www.crystalclarity.com

To request a catalog, place an order for the above products, or to find out more information, please contact us at:

Crystal Clarity Publishers
14618 Tyler Foote Rd., Nevada City, CA 95959
phone: 800.424.1055 or 530.478.7600
email: clarity@crystalclarity.com
fax: 530.478.7610

Crystal Clarity also offers all music and audiobook downloads from all the popular music and audiobook websites.

Ananda Worldwide

Ananda Sangha, a worldwide organization founded by Swami Kriyananda, offers spiritual support and resources based on the teachings of Paramhansa Yogananda. For more information about Ananda Sangha, communities, or meditation groups near you, please call or visit them on the web at:

530.478.7560 • www.ananda.org

The Expanding Light

Ananda's guest retreat, *The Expanding Light,* offers a varied, year round schedule of classes and workshops on yoga, meditation, and spiritual practice. You may also come for a relaxed personal renewal, participating in ongoing activities as much or as little as you wish.

The beautiful serene mountain setting, supportive staff, and delicious vegetarian food provide an ideal environment for a truly meaningful, spiritual vacation. For more information about *The Expanding Light Yoga and Mediation Retreat* and its programs, please call or visit them on the web at:

800.346.5350 • www.expandinglight.org